SHEDDING OUR STARS

THE STORY OF HANS CALMEYER AND HOW HE SAVED THOUSANDS OF FAMILIES LIKE MINE

LAUREEN NUSSBAUM

with KAREN KIRTLEY

PRAISE FOR *SHEDDING OUR STARS*

✠ ✠ ✠

"Thanks to Ursula LeGuin, I came aboard this powerful vessel: an inspirational story, largely unknown, of the Jews of Holland, the incredible role of the young German official Hans Calmeyer, and the many thousands of lives he saved. Stories of Anne Frank's family, and Laureen and Rudi Nussbaum's own stories. Even a story of my own family. Of all our families, I was in tears again and again."

—DR. TONY WOLK, Professor of English, Portland State University, and author of *The Parable of You* and the Lincoln Out of Time trilogy

"What is the price of integrity? In occupied Holland, the German bureaucrat Hans Calmeyer (1903–1972) saved at least 3,700 Jewish lives and protected 9,000 more in mixed marriages. After 1945, some Germans saw him as a traitor, or self-serving. Laureen Nussbaum, who grew up with Anne and Margot Frank, was among the lucky ones able to remove the yellow star thanks to Calmeyer. Nussbaum's account proves we need eye-witness testimony to take heed of the past and its legacy in the present."

—DR. PENNY MILBOUER, translator of *Between Persecution and Participation: Biography of a Bookkeeper at J. A. Topf & Söhne*

"This is an inspiring story of quiet resistance from a German lawyer, Hans Calmeyer, who, while playing his role as a loyal German in the 'dejudification' of the Netherlands, maintained a rescue operation that saved thousands of Jewish lives, more than Schindler. Among them was Laureen Nussbaum, whose account in this remarkable biography/autobiography is like that of Anne

Frank, her friend, in rendering the feel and texture of living in Amsterdam during the war. . . . Gripping and revelatory."
—DR. GAYLE GREENE, author of *The Woman Who Knew Too Much: Alice Stewart and the Secrets of Radiation* and *Missing Persons: A Memoir*

"This intertwined family memoir and Calmeyer biography gives a unique take on a familiar story. It reads like a novel, showing how two people—a fourteen-year-old girl who was helping her boyfriend in hiding, and a German bureaucrat who was saving lives under constant scrutiny—managed to resist the Nazis. You'll see the world of Nazi-occupied Amsterdam in more intimate detail than ever before—and unlike a novel, you'll see what happens to the author and Calmeyer after the war years were over. We need this book now, for its example of two people of unimpeachable integrity in the worst of times, and for its warning."
—MARY DINGEE FILLMORE, author of *An Address in Amsterdam*

SHEDDING OUR STARS

SHEDDING OUR STARS

THE STORY OF HANS CALMEYER
AND HOW HE SAVED THOUSANDS
OF FAMILIES LIKE MINE

✣ ✣ ✣

LAUREEN NUSSBAUM
WITH KAREN KIRTLEY

SHE WRITES PRESS

Published October 2019
Printed in the United States of America
Print ISBN: 978-1-63152-636-7
E-ISBN: 978-1-63152-637-4
Library of Congress Control Number: 2019940523

For information, address:
She Writes Press
1569 Solano Ave #546
Berkeley, CA 94707

Interior design by Tabitha Lahr

She Writes Press is a division of SparkPoint Studio, LLC.

Unless otherwise noted, all translations from the German and the Dutch are by Laureen Nussbaum, and all illustrations, except otherwise stated, are her property.

Dedicated to the memory of Calmeyer's biographer, Peter Niebaum, and to those born after us, especially to Hans Calmeyer's offspring: Micah Victoria, Alexander Hannes, and Nicholas Albrecht Hentschel, the children of his son Michael Calmeyer Hentschel.

For a person who was "Aryanized," the gate to life opened.
—BENNO STOKVIS, 1961, Dutch lawyer in
the occupation years

Too little, too little!
—HANS CALMEYER, 1965, letter to Dr. J. Presser

Contents

❖ ❖ ❖

Introduction by Ted Koppel

✛ ✛ ✛

I have always been vaguely familiar with the theory of six degrees of separation—the notion that each of us is somehow connected, however tenuously, with any other person on the planet through a chain of no more than five intermediaries. It is easily demonstrable when the first link in the chain has been a journalist for more than fifty years. Having met Nelson Mandela, Mikhail Gorbachev, Ronald Reagan, among several thousand other newsmakers, my "connection" to the millions, the hundreds of millions who swirled in and out of their collective orbits, is only a single point of separation away. Multiplied four more times by successive layers of intermediaries and arithmetic does the rest. Unaware as we may be, we are, at least mathematically speaking, demonstrably connected to one another. It is a small world.

Curiously, I need no such device to link me to the hero of this book, although his name and, indeed, his very existence, were unknown to me until Laureen Nussbaum asked me to write this introduction. Laureen's mother, Marianne, and mine, Alice, were close friends as young German women in Frankfurt/Main between the two world wars. They remained so throughout the turbulent decades that followed. It is difficult to imagine now, in the knowledge of what was to come, but the sense of identity that characterized these two young women centered more on their nationality than their religion. The fact that Marianne was raised a Christian and Alice was Jewish had no more impact on their friendship during the years of the Weimar Republic in Germany than a similar relationship would experience these days in the United States. Indeed, Marianne soon married a Jew, Joseph Klein.

To a much greater degree than their eastern European co-religionists, German Jews were assimilated. My father, Erwin Koppel, served four years in the German army during the First World War. In light of all that would ultimately transpire under the Nazis, it now seems relatively trivial, but many years later my father would recall how shattered he was to find that he had been declared stateless. He had always been, he believed, a totally committed German. Germany's Jews during the Weimar Republic were, they believed, inextricably woven into the fabric of their nation's culture and society. Walther Rathenau served as Germany's first Jewish foreign minister almost fifty years before Henry Kissinger earned a similar distinction as the U.S. Secretary of State. Recalling my father's sense of nationalism, I can only imagine the growing sense of despair that ultimately convinced him to flee Germany and move to England in 1937. He and my mother, Alice Neu, had been "keeping company" (in the delicate euphemism of those times) for a number of years but did not marry until well after she joined him in Lancashire, England, in 1938. Marianne Klein visited them there in August 1939, half a year before I was born.

The Kleins and their three daughters had taken refuge in Holland several years earlier. The Kleins and the Koppels would not see one another again until July 1948, at which time the author of this book, Laureen Nussbaum, was still known by the diminutive of her given German name, Hannelore—Hansi. As a pre-pubescent at the time, I was only vaguely aware of the circumstances that threw Hansi and the dark, somewhat brooding, Rudi Nussbaum together. I knew that Rudi had been given shelter by the Kleins during the Nazi occupation of Holland. I never quite understood how it was that the Kleins were in a position to give anyone shelter. Hansi's father, Joseph, after all, was himself a Jew. The three girls, under the principles of Aryan purity that governed life in Germany, would surely also have been considered Jews, their Christian grandmother notwithstanding. Rudi's survival of the war and ultimately his marriage to Hansi seemed simply a happier version of the far better-known story of Anne Frank, whose diary and ultimate death in a Nazi concentration camp have become the universal chronicle of the Holocaust, writ small.

I never knew, until reading the first chapter of this book, that the Kleins and the Franks had been friends in Frankfurt, had attended the same synagogue, moved to the same neighborhood in Amsterdam. I am removed from Anne Frank, I discover, by only one degree of separation. How extraordinary to learn this only now, near the end of my own passage through life. Even so, the nagging question of how the Kleins were in a position to offer shelter to young Rudi Nussbaum, given their own vulnerability to the Nazi selection process, has only been clarified by this touching and illuminating introduction to what may seem an oxymoron: a heroic bureaucrat.

Hans Calmeyer, easily overlooked as a functionary in the Nazi machine, was, you will learn, a hero of epic proportions, risking his own security to save the lives of thousands of Jews. Among those, a Jewish woman who once served as his secretary married, it turns out, to a Heinz Koppel. What, if any, relationship exists between Heinz and me I may never know. It is only one in a series of bewildering discoveries, among which is the extraordinarily gratifying one that permits me to claim, with pride, that Hans Calmeyer and I are linked by merely one degree of separation.

We live, once again, in perilous times when millions of people have been uprooted by war and brutal prejudice to navigate the shoals of general, global indifference. Hans Calmeyer would, I think, be proud of Angela Merkel's principled offer of refuge to so many hundreds of thousands of desperate Muslims; just as we Americans will, I believe, one day cringe in shame at our failure to match Germany's generosity of spirit.

That, however, is the subject of another book for another day.

—TED KOPPEL
Potomac, MD, spring 2016

PREFACE

✤ ✤ ✤

In 1992, the exhibition *Anne Frank in the World* came to Portland, Oregon, where my husband and I had made our home for over thirty years. The exhibition was a major event. Some two dozen people in the greater Portland area who had lived through the Holocaust were willing to speak about their experiences. They told their stories and answered questions, bringing seventy-two thousand visitors closer to what had happened in Europe under the Nazi regime half a century earlier. I was one of those witnesses.

In 1936, my parents emigrated with their three daughters from Frankfurt/Main to Amsterdam. We, the Kleins, settled in the same neighborhood as Anne Frank's family, whom we had known in Frankfurt. Margot Frank, Anne's older sister, was among the first four thousand Jewish refugees aged sixteen to forty ordered to report for "forced labor" in Germany. My older sister was served the same summons. Anne had just turned thirteen, I was almost fifteen, and my younger sister twelve, all three of us too young under the edict to be sent away.

It is well known from Anne's diary that the day after Margot received the summons, the Frank family went into hiding in the back quarters of Otto Frank's business. They managed to hold out for twenty-five months, thanks to the loving care of Mr. Frank's clerical staff and to the unwavering support of his business partners. Anne wrote vividly about their secret life above the office and warehouse rooms.

Sadly, Otto Frank was the only one in the family to survive the war. Anne and Margot died from typhus at Bergen-Belsen, and Mrs. Frank succumbed to exhaustion in Auschwitz. Upon his return to Amsterdam, despite his tremendous loss, Mr. Frank was happy to find that his business partners and his office staff had survived the horrors, and that my family still lived in the same apartment where he had last visited us three years before.

How had we escaped the dance of death, he'd asked at the time, a question repeated again and again whenever I speak about the Holocaust. There were other "good" Germans besides Oskar Schindler with his now-famous list. Thanks to one of them, a little-known lawyer named Hans Calmeyer, my family and thousands of other Jews survived.

As one who benefited from Calmeyer's courage, I have long felt the urge to write his story in English. I base this on sources in German and in Dutch, primarily on the biographical works by Peter Niebaum but also on the books by the lawyers Mathias Middelberg and Ruth van Galen-Herrmann. The result is this biography of an unsung hero, a man who never joined the Nazi party and who took enormous risks in his position at the headquarters of the German High Commissioner in the Netherlands to sabotage Hitler's "final solution."

Hans Calmeyer saved the lives of more Jews than Schindler. Among many others, my family and I owe Calmeyer a great and unpayable debt. Without him, we wouldn't be here. I fervently hope that this book, which blends my family's story with his, will help to bring him the international recognition he is due.

Chapter One

EARLY CHILDHOOD
IN FRANKFURT

✣ ✣ ✣

I was only five years old when Hitler became chancellor of Germany on January 30, 1933. Yet, I have vivid memories of countless SA units (*Sturmabteilung*, Nazi Stormtroopers) marching in their mustard-colored uniforms through the streets of Frankfurt, singing Nazi propaganda songs. One day my parents caught me parading in a similar fashion along the long corridor from the front of our apartment to the kitchen. I had my father's cane slung over my right shoulder in lieu of a rifle, and I was singing *"Die Fahne hoch"* (Hold up the Flag), one of the most popular Nazi songs. My dismayed parents made me stop immediately and forbade me from ever again marching in that fashion.

At the time, I was too young to understand the implications of Hitler's takeover, but my parents were well aware of the ominous portent as the Nazis spouted their anti-Semitic propaganda and clamped down systematically on anything leftist, Marxist, or even pacifist.

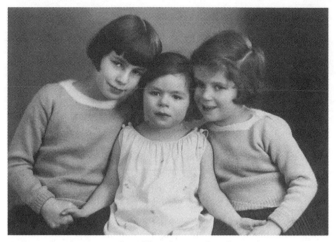

Susanne (Susi), Marion (Marli) and Hannelore (Hansi) Klein, 1932

My early childhood had been stable and comfortable, idyllic in its innocence, but the world around us was changing rapidly. The decade prior to my birth had been difficult for Germany. The Treaty of Versailles, signed June 18, 1919, put an end to the German Empire in the wake of its defeat in World War I. The victorious powers radically reduced the territory of the newly created democratic German republic, called the Weimar Republic for the town where its liberal constitution was written. The treaty imposed harsh reparations, leaving the Germans with a rising tower of debt and a bitter sense of unjust punishment.

By 1923, the year my parents married, German war reparations payments were in arrears and the economy was failing. Hyperinflation drove up the price of bread to two hundred million marks by November, leaving most families in ruins. Germany's right-wing political parties, including Hitler's Nazi Party (officially the NSDAP, or National Socialist German Labor Party), promised restoration of German pride, quick and radical change, and an end to economic misery.

Hitler persuaded many with his populist speeches that he could fix everything quickly and that the future belonged to a new Germany. His party was founded in 1920 with a group of sixty-four supporters. Three years later, more than fifty thousand Nazi party members rallied in Munich under the swastika flag for the first national party convention.

Boycotts against Jewish-owned businesses began shortly after the National Socialists took over. In May of 1933, Nazis publicly burned books written by Jewish authors as well as by pacifists, communists, and socialists in a nationwide "action against the un-German Spirit."

The democratic republic established in Weimar, a constitutional state, was rapidly undone. The Nazi "Enabling Act" banned the Communist and the Socialist parties; the *Gleichschaltung* (enforced alignment) of the trade unions and the press was implemented. Stormtroopers were in evidence all over the country. Hermann Göring and Heinrich Himmler set up the Gestapo, the secret state police.

Jews and anti-fascists began leaving Germany in response to the dictatorial control by the Nazi party. Many of them left their home country to or via the Netherlands. Those who emigrated earliest fared best economically, because they were permitted to take their assets and their belongings. Over the course of the 1930s, the restrictions tightened. Some of the people who left were friends from my father's liberal Westend Synagogue. These included the Frank family. Anne Frank's *Diary* later became famous worldwide for its compelling account of life in hiding during the Holocaust.

My parents considered themselves thoroughly assimilated into German society. My Jewish father was a financial expert in a large metal firm. My mother's father was also Jewish, but he'd had little influence on her upbringing. She'd been raised for six years in a Protestant foster family and later by her Catholic

Marianne Klein, mid 1930s

Joseph Klein, mid 1930s

mother. We celebrated Hanukkah at home and Christmas at my maternal grandmother's. Our family was well established in Frankfurt, and my parents treasured the cultural life in the city. They had no desire to leave. Like many other people at the time, they saw the barbarism of the Nazis as a temporary aberration. They couldn't imagine that Hitler would last.

Yet, by the end of 1935, my parents were convinced that we needed to leave Frankfurt. In the previous two years, the life we'd shared there as a family had been taken away from us bit by bit. Public schools were segregated. Bernhard Rust, Germany's National Secretary of Education, proclaimed, "One of the basic conditions for successful educational work is racial conformity between teacher and student. Children of Jewish descent are very detrimental to the homogeneity of the classroom and to the unhampered realization of national-socialist education of our youth."[1]

At the time, I was a third grader. My elementary school had enough Jewish students to set apart one wing of the building with a separate entrance for us. It hurt when Elfriede Kunz, a non-Jewish girl with whom I used to walk to school, steered clear of me. Even worse were the horribly anti-Semitic cartoons in *Der Stürmer* (The Assailer) in the newsstand I passed on my way to school.

Since we were banished from joining our contemporaries in sports and games, many of us Jewish children compensated for our exclusion by getting together in small groups to learn Hebrew songs and to practice dancing the *horah*, the Jewish line dance. At school our class performed a play, *The Princess with the Nose*, about an insolent princess magically cured of her bad behavior with wine from Israel.[2]

Even the very naïve in mid-1930s Germany could no longer doubt that they were living under a dictator whose word was to be the law of the land. In 1935, at the NSDAP party rally in Nuremberg, it was announced that marriages between Jews and Aryans (non-Jews) were forbidden. So was extramarital intercourse between Jews and citizens of German or kindred blood.

The uncertainties of starting over in another country, many though they were, finally tallied as less than the very real risk to our lives if we remained in Germany. Some of our friends had already left, and many were to follow. I looked forward to the adventure of living in a new country and learning a new language, but my older sister, Susi, who was part of a group of close friends, felt desolate as they scattered across the globe. Marli (family nickname for our youngest sister, Marion) was not quite six and too young to voice an opinion.

Chapter Two

HANS CALMEYER

✤ ✤ ✤

Little did I know that, while I was in kindergarten getting ready
to go to school, a young lawyer who would later have a profound
impact on me and my family was just starting his career in
another German city.

Hans Calmeyer was born June 23, 1903, in Osnabrück, a
city in northwest Germany roughly halfway between Berlin and
Amsterdam. His mother, Elisabeth Abeken, came from a highly
respected patrician family that had lived in Osnabrück for centuries. His father, Georg Rudolf Calmeyer, a judge, hailed from
a family of landowners and businessmen in Gehrde, a village to
the north of Osnabrück.

Hans was the youngest of three boys. He adored his older
brothers Alfred and Rudel and relied on their example and
advice. Temperamentally they could hardly have been more different. Alfred was rational and judicious, Rudel impetuous and
artistic. Hans came to see himself as an amalgam of the two:
from an early age he was both dutiful and fanciful, a reliable and
systematic worker as well as a dreamer. The Calmeyer brothers
grew up in a comfortable, upper-middle-class neighborhood.

Next door lived the prominent Westerkamp family. Eberhard was Hans's friend from infancy. Their nannies walked the boys out in their buggies together.[1]

Hans Calmeyer as a school boy in Gnesen, 1914

Father Calmeyer's career as a judge took the family to Gnesen (Gniezno in Polish), in the province of Posen, the town where Polish kings had been crowned during the Middle Ages. Poland's borders with neighboring Prussia, Austria, and Russia had been redrawn several times over the preceding 150 years, as the country was partitioned and repartitioned after a series of wars. Gnesen was Prussian from 1814 until the end of World War I in 1919, when it once again became Gniezno, in reconstituted Poland. The town's fraught history left its population rife with cultural, ideological, and ethnic divisions. As an adolescent, Hans Calmeyer was sensitive to the tensions and found himself siding with the weaker minorities, Poles and Jews, against the dominant Prussians with their nationalist-militarist traditions.

World War I broke out in 1914, when Hans's older brothers

were in their mid-teens. They served in the German Army late in the war. In the space of a few days in April 1918, the Calmeyer brothers were both killed in action in Flanders, northern France. His brothers' deaths on the battlefield marked the end of childhood for Hans, who was not yet fifteen years old.[2]

As a young law student in Munich, Calmeyer found himself tangentially involved in the unsuccessful coup attempt to overthrow the government of Bavaria that became known as the Beer Hall Putsch of 1923. On November 9, Hitler and General Erich Ludendorff, a highly esteemed strategist of the German Army during World War I, led some three thousand marchers through the streets of central Munich toward the *Feldherrnhalle* (literally, the General's Hall). Calmeyer accompanied a student company of the Black *Reichswehr*, an illegal offshoot of the former German Army, mostly consisting of disbanded reserve units and volunteer militias.

As the front ranks of marchers surged toward the heart of the city, Munich police blocked their way. Calmeyer and his fellow students watched from afar as a skirmish broke out between the *Landespolizei* (Bavarian police) and the Nazi rebels. Hitler and many of his Nazi cohorts fled the scene. Ludendorff calmly led the remaining marchers toward a nearby square, where he and other leaders of the putsch were arrested.

In the fall of 1946, recalling the putsch, Calmeyer wrote emphatically that he was with the student militia, "but not as a follower of Hitler." Referring to himself in the third person, he went on to say: "In fact, the experience of the day separated the young activist—whom even then some of his contemporaries called an incurable idealist and jurist—from many friends and decisively from any kind of nationalism."[3] Thereafter his sympathies lay firmly with the Independent Socialist Party of Germany (the USPD), which had no nationalistic overtones.

After studying at several different universities, Calmeyer enrolled at Friedrich Schiller University in Jena in 1924. Here his aspirations and study habits gelled, and his grades were excellent. In his journal, the young law student sought to understand himself and others. Driven by ambition and pride, he alternated between states of exuberance, emphatic affirmations of life, moments of self-satisfaction and states of deep despair, anxiety before examinations, profound insecurities, and harsh self-criticism.

His favorite book was Thomas Mann's new novel, *The Magic Mountain*. In its protagonist, Hans Castorp, he saw himself. He commented in his diary:

> It hurts me daily to find myself totally unable to express what flashes through my mind. If only I could be rid of it. Instead, all the experiences of the last eight years that I have stored within me, weigh painfully on me. They are shadows I cannot banish. I love these shadows and undergo the anguish as a kind of happiness, to which I revert time and again. Every memory includes anguish, because it always contains something lost, something irretrievable, something to weep for.
>
> In *The Magic Mountain*: "Passion is to live for the sake of life. You people, however, live for the sake of experiences. Passion, that is, forgetting oneself. You people, however, are after enriching yourselves."
>
> ... It is all right to substitute love for life, possibly even makes things clearer both for Hans Castorp and for myself.[4]

In *Ein anderer Deutscher* (A Different Kind of German), Calmeyer's biographer Peter Niebaum included quotations from the young law student's journal that foreshadow the mature Calmeyer. In the first one Hans asks himself what would make for a truly good person.

The answer: one who is characterized by kindness.

In the second entry he notes, "Yet, there are ridiculously small things that are possibly bigger than great heroic deeds. They do not inspire awe; on the contrary, they appear pitiful and foolish—and yet they are informed by more intrinsic, intimate values. (Hasn't somebody already described such heroes?)"[5]

Hans Calmeyer as a law student, early 1920s

Calmeyer sailed through his first national law examination at the end of 1925 and launched into the three and a half years of internship required of prospective lawyers.

He met Ruth Labusch in Jena in 1926. She was two and a half years younger than he. Ruth shared Hans's left-liberal political convictions and never hesitated to lambast those she disagreed with. The two were passionately drawn to each other and began a romantic, often tempestuous relationship that ebbed and flowed but endured to the end of his life.

Theirs was an unlikely match. Where Hans was patient, perceptive, and tactful, Ruth was brutally blunt. Where he sometimes dithered, over-rationalized or withdrew into reverie, she got right to the point and acted decisively, leaving burned bridges behind her. Hans admired Ruth's fiery nature and firmness of mind; yet all too often he found her ill-humored and disagreeable. Between quarrels and reconciliations over the next two years, they became engaged.

An important way station in Calmeyer's legal education was the appellate court in the town of Celle. There Hans roomed with a colleague from Osnabrück named Wilhelm Rosebrock. The two men formed an intense and long-lasting friendship. A joke between them was that when they were hanged, it would have to be from the same tree.

Rosebrock gives a description of the young Calmeyer:

A gentleman of the old school, courtly in his manners, but beneath this surface a leftist rebel, enthusiastic about the USPD [the Independent Socialist Party of Germany]. In the presence of the wrong people, he can simply turn to ice. Otherwise he loves eloquent language, as I do. Moreover, an intelligent fellow, tolerant, liberal, a considerable legal talent—only too generous with money. Intellectually at all times a most stimulating man, who can also step back. . . . Hans Calmeyer is amiability personified. With his fiancée I have a problem, though: Ruth is terribly high-strung.[6]

Calmeyer passed his second national law examination in 1929 and became a fully accredited lawyer. The following year he married Ruth with little fanfare. A baby was on the way.

Calmeyer assumed his first professional position as a clerk assessor for the public prosecutor in Halle, on the Saale River. Ruth was heavily pregnant when they arrived; their son Peter was born there on September 5, 1930. Calmeyer quickly realized that his calling was to defend rather than to prosecute, and he soon left the job.

He worried about the increasing strength of the Nazi Party. In 1930, the party doubled the number of its seats in the *Reichstag*, the German parliament. Hitler drew crowds to grandly staged rallies where he thundered promises to undo the humiliation of the Treaty of Versailles and restore the former glory of the Fatherland. His party, he pledged, would disprove the lie that Germany had caused the outbreak of World War I. The aggressor was not the noble German nation, but a cabal of Jews, socialists, and communists.

Hans and Ruth Calmeyer in the Osnabrück house, early 1930s

Calmeyer knew that as a public officer he would have to follow Hitler's orders if the Nazi Party came to power. Thus in 1931 he returned to his home city to open a private law office. In Osnabrück, the Calmeyers moved in circles bound together by a critical appraisal of the Nazis and by a love of the arts. Close friends included Josef Woldering, a banker motivated by his Roman Catholic worldview, and Bruno Hanckel, a bookseller who promoted leftist socialist ideas. To the dismay of all, the tide of popular support for Hitler steadily rose. When Hitler made a public appearance in Osnabrück in the summer of 1932, a local dignitary welcomed him with a strongly anti-Semitic speech. The event drew an audience of 25,000 people, over a quarter of the town's population.[7]

Calmeyer's childhood friend Eberhard Westerkamp became the district president, an important administrator in the local government. Embracing the new regime, Westerkamp professed allegiance to National Socialism: "It is now my firm intent to work in the spirit of this great time with my whole heart and with sincere affirmation of the new epoch. . . . National Socialism has outgrown the party system. It will comprise all Germans."[8]

Despite his new fealty to the Nazi Party, Westerkamp declared himself in favor of religious tolerance and against total centralization of state power, much to his credit in Calmeyer's view.

Calmeyer went his own way. He employed a Jewish secretary, Henny Hirsch, a count against him by Nazi reckoning. He belonged to no political party, but he occasionally defended communists arrested during altercations with the Nazis. Ruth drew attention as a vocal opponent of Nazi doctrine. For all these reasons, Calmeyer's office came under a cloud of suspicion in a town where Hitler was popular.

In the autumn of 1933, Calmeyer's license to plead at the bar of both the local court and the appellate court was temporarily revoked in retaliation for having defended communists. That meant he could no longer practice his profession. A later decree made the suspension permanent. Local Nazis had branded Calmeyer a "parlor Bolshevist" and deemed him untrustworthy.

Joined by other influential friends, District President Westerkamp interceded with the SS (*Schutzstaffel*, the Nazi Party's security service), on Calmeyer's behalf, declaring him a sentimental, humanitarian idealist, yet an excellent jurist who would be an asset for the National Socialist movement.

After six months of professional ostracism, Calmeyer was readmitted to the bar and again allowed to work as a lawyer. The reasons for the Nazis' change of heart remain obscure, but family legend holds forth the following curious tale.

Anti-militarist Calmeyer avidly collected hand-painted, miniature tin soldiers. In his months of unemployment, he visited an exhibition of tin soldiers in Hanover. The showcases featured reconstructions of Napoleon's battles. A fellow collector overheard Calmeyer grumbling to himself, "That is incorrect. The cavalry is not properly aligned; the artillery is not correct either."

The onlooker readily agreed and struck up a conversation, during which Calmeyer mentioned his precarious professional situation. His interlocutor, who turned out to be the brother of Prussian Minister of Justice Hanns Kerrl, opined, "I must discuss your case with my brother. It does not stand to reason that a man who is so knowledgeable about Napoleon's battles would be infected by Communism."[9]

Readmission to the bar did not end Calmeyer's vexations. The Nazi block warden kept a watchful eye on his family. The Gestapo searched their house, expecting to find the works of Marx or Engels, but left empty-handed. When Calmeyer's young son Peter became ill, a doctor refused to treat him, saying his services were not available to "Jew-lovers."

The Calmeyers considered emigration but were dissuaded by a Dutch cousin, Michael Callmeyer [correctly spelled with a double "l"], who convinced them it was wiser to stay in place. The German government would see emigration as treason, and those who left would never be able to return to their native country.

Calmeyer later recalled his own reasoning:

> Emigration is either the loss of one's homeland, or it may even force the political activist into the service of another nation. However, service to and pay by another nation make it impossible for him to address fellow countrymen as compatriots. For a spirited young man, it remains a depressing and terrible task to do no more than assume the warning role of a Cassandra and point out to his country-men—deluded by economic upswing and public assistance—the inescapable consequence of military rearmament and the accompanying juridical and moral disarmament of which these countrymen are unaware. It is a depressing and terrible task to point this out in vain, time and again in vain.[10]

In retrospect, Calmeyer's decision to stay in Germany was providentially the right one. Refugee lawyers had a particularly hard time finding their bearings in overseas countries, since their knowledge and degrees were nontransferable, and refugees who returned to their home country after Hitler was defeated were not welcome, nor did they fit into postwar Germany. Most importantly, though: who would have been assigned Calmeyer's wartime job in the Netherlands, and what would have been the ramifications for thousands of Jews, had he not been the one in charge of "doubtful cases"?

Chapter Three

Settling in the Netherlands

✤ ✤ ✤

I was eight years old when my family emigrated to the Netherlands in April 1936. My parents found an apartment in the southern part of Amsterdam, the River District, where hundreds of Jewish refugees settled. Though smaller and much more modest than our Frankfurt apartment, which covered a whole floor of a large house, our new home was in a neighborhood of brand-new blocks of four-story apartment buildings, many with central heat and hot water, at the time a novelty in Holland. The rent for these apartments was too high for the average Dutch family, since in the Netherlands, as in Germany, unemployment was rampant during the Great Depression of the mid-1930s. Yet many middle-class emigrant families, who had left Germany early enough, had been allowed to take along their furniture and some of their money. They could afford the rents.

From late April to summer vacation, my older sister and I went to "transition school," where we learned the Dutch language, history, and geography. The following September, the director of the transition classes advised the parents of refugee youngsters to have their children set back one year, so they could ease in. That is what happened to most of my fellow students, but I insisted on going into fourth grade. My older sister allowed herself to be placed two grades lower than she should have been and found herself just one year ahead of me instead of three. The consequences for her and for our family dynamics were profound. Susi was no longer the undisputed oldest. Rather, the two of us were the big girls and Marli the little one.

I am fairly sure that during my family's early days in Amsterdam, Otto Frank, who had come with his family two and a half years before us, advised my father as to how to set up a wholesale business in clothing accessories and notions such as buttons, belts, and buckles. In the late 1930s, my father undertook long business trips to the Middle East and South Africa to market these items.

In 1938 my maternal grandmother, whom we called "Omi," also moved to Amsterdam. She found an apartment around the corner from us. Omi had many friends and led her own life, but as the years wore on, she had dinner with us every night.

The author's grandmother, "Omi," with her fox-terrier, late 1930s

My sisters and I attended municipal schools along with Margot and Anne Frank. My age was between those of the two Frank girls, a year and a half younger than Margot and two years older than Anne. All of us youngsters relished our newfound freedom in the Netherlands, where we could ride our bikes and go anywhere without bumping into restrictions placed on Jews.

Margot Frank, school photo, 1941

Hansje (Hannelore) Klein, school photo, 1941

Anne Frank, school photo, 1941

There was no government-decreed anti-Semitism in the Netherlands. We were young enough to learn Dutch with ease, while our parents had to ask us how to say things in Dutch. We would correct them, wagging our forefingers. "No, you cannot say it that way. It should be such and such." Soon we knew Dutch history as well as any of our classmates and were at home with Dutch geography. In our minds we were little Dutch girls.

When we arrived in 1936, Amsterdam was a city with 800,000 inhabitants, 30 percent Protestant, 30 percent Roman Catholic, 30 percent without religious affiliation, and 10 percent Jewish. Dutch Jews were either Orthodox or unaffiliated. My father, the Franks, and other Jewish immigrant families founded a liberal Jewish Congregation, with a synagogue in the Tolstraat, just north of the River District.

Margot, my sister Susi, and I biked together to our Wednesday afternoon *Joodse les* (Jewish classes), where we read the stories of the Old Testament and learned the Hebrew alphabet so we could follow the prayers and blessings during services. We did not really study the Hebrew language beyond rote memorization and translation of the most frequent incantations. Anne and Marli were too young to partake of our Jewish education, but they came to the children's celebrations of some of the Jewish holidays. At these occasions, Mrs. Frank was quite active in the congregation.

Despite the reports from loved ones back in Germany, the next few years of my childhood in Amsterdam were rich and full. Unlike the adults, I did not dwell on the growing Nazi conflict, focusing instead on my studies and my hobbies, especially playing soccer with the neighborhood boys. However, it was just a matter of time before even the youngest among us were impacted again by the Nazis' determination to rule Europe.

When the German Army marched into Poland, my father realized our safety was again in jeopardy. With the help of a cousin who lived in Montevideo, he tried to secure the necessary papers to move the family to Uruguay. But before we could get the coveted visas, the German Army invaded the Netherlands in May 1940. They quickly overwhelmed the Dutch military and sealed the borders. Thus began the Nazi occupation, a devastating time for most Dutch people, especially for the Jews.

Vivid memories of the German invasion are still with me. My family lived at the southern edge of Amsterdam. From our attic window we could see German war planes dropping bombs on Schiphol, the Amsterdam airport—the searchlights, tracer fire, explosions in the air. There was no basement under our apartment building, but we were required by the Air Raid Department to repair to the first floor, at street level, and sit out the time between the warning siren and the all-clear signal.

I also remember with a shudder the many suicides in our block once the Dutch Army capitulated. Quite a number of our neighbors were Jewish refugees from Germany and Austria. Some had already been in Buchenwald or other concentration camps. They jumped to their deaths rather than submit once again to the tender mercies of the Nazis.

Meanwhile, just days before Hitler ordered the invasion of Poland and World War II began, Hans Calmeyer was drafted into military service. He was ordered to sign up for an SS reserve unit but opted instead to join the *Flugwachekommando*

Hans Calmeyer between two other members of his unit, 1940

(FLUKO), formerly a paramilitary organization scanning the skies for intruding airplanes. It had recently been taken over by the *Luftwaffe* (German Air Force). At air-defense posts around the country, observers searched the sky and telephoned reports of suspected enemy aircraft to area reporting centers of the FLUKO, whose evaluators tried to make sense of incoming reports. When staff members of the Osnabrück FLUKO center were asked who might want to move to a more westerly post closer to the Dutch border, Hans Calmeyer was among those who volunteered.

On May 16, 1940, following the surrender of the Dutch Army, Calmeyer's FLUKO team was sent across the border.[1] The unit was billeted to the southeast of Rotterdam, in the area between Dordrecht and Breda. Calmeyer was a reluctant soldier. A Dutch friend once asked him what he would do if he were sent to France. He had a ready answer: "I can always hold my rifle so high that my bullets will not hit any Frenchman."[2]

Chapter Four

THE FIRST YEARS OF
GERMAN OCCUPATION

✤ ✤ ✤

In the beginning, our life under German occupation seemed to go on much as before. The Germans considered the Dutch fellow Aryans, whose hearts and minds they hoped to win. After vanquishing the Allies, they intended to incorporate the Netherlands into the German Reich. Moreover, several German authorities had assured the mayor of Amsterdam and other officials that no actions had been planned against the Jewish population of the Netherlands.[1]

Even so, the first decree publicly discriminating against Jews was promulgated by the German authorities as early as July of 1940. All Jews were expelled from the Dutch Air Raid Department, along with other "undesirable elements" who might harbor anti-German sentiment.

Among the immigrants who had arrived in Amsterdam after us were the Nussbaums. They had belonged to the same liberal Jewish congregation in Frankfurt as the Franks and my family. Mr. Nussbaum, an accredited pharmacist in Germany, opened a small drugstore on our block. He and his teenaged son Rudi were fine musicians. They often came to our apartment to play chamber music with my mother or sing *Lieder* (art songs) by Franz Schubert, Hugo Wolf, and other German and Austrian composers.

Since my mother had been part of the *Wandervögel* (birds of passage) movement as a teenager in Vienna, she was quite progressive with regard to girls and boys going on weekend hikes together in the countryside. The *Wandervögel* had been organized at the turn of the twentieth century as a reaction to the materialism, hypocrisy, and stifling conservatism of the Kaiser Reich, values usually called "Victorian" in Anglo-Saxon countries. It was a back-to-nature movement emphasizing freedom, self-responsibility, and the spirit of adventure. Mother had no objections when, in the summer of 1940, my older sister, Susi, and I wanted to go on a camping vacation with Rudi Nussbaum and his friend Rolf Schwarz.

We biked to the province of Gelderland, some fifty miles east of Amsterdam, and slept in the hayloft of a Jewish farmer. A blanket hanging from a beam divided the boys' quarters from the girls'. We cooked over an open fire and spent our days bicycling in the Royal Forests, where in hushed silence we watched deer grazing in the clearings and wild boars rooting in the thickets. To stretch our food allowance, we picked huckleberries and gathered mushrooms, and we thoroughly enjoyed what we feared might be our last carefree summer break.

School resumed in September. I was in eighth grade, Susi in ninth. Rudi was doing his second and last year at the School for Ship Engineers, where he was one of three or four Jewish students. Rolf, who was already twenty, returned to his temporary technical job.

Several families, including ours and the Franks, hired a refugee journalist from Berlin to tutor a group of teenagers in German literature. The aim was to supplement their education, as well as to give work to another recent German immigrant in the Netherlands. Margot Frank and Susi belonged to the group, and so did Rudi, at least in the beginning. At age thirteen, I was deemed too young to join them, but I sat in whenever the group met at our house. We read the German classics: plays by Lessing, Goethe, and Schiller, all focusing on tolerance and freedom. Little did I know that I would be teaching some of these same plays decades later in the United States! I remember admiring Margot Frank. She was older than I and physically more mature, quiet and ladylike, while I was a lively tomboy.

That autumn, the Germans decreed that Jewish public servants could no longer be promoted, nor could Jews be appointed to public service. Shortly afterward, all Jewish public servants were summarily dismissed. As a young teen I was mostly unaware of these ominous restrictions. I remember that the winter of 1940–1941 was a cold one. We did a great deal of skating on the canals, swirling along in a happy crowd.

In January 1941, every Jew in the Netherlands had to fill out a special form stating how many Jewish grandparents he or she had. People did as they were told. In retrospect I wonder why, by and large, the Jews were so law abiding. There were protests, particularly from non-Jewish people. Several professors at the University of Leiden resigned their positions when their Jewish colleagues were dismissed, and students at the Technical Institute of Higher Learning in Delft went on a protest strike. The German authorities closed both schools.[2]

More and more hotels, cafés, and restaurants allowed themselves to be bullied into posting the sign *Voor Joden verboden* (Not for Jews). In early 1941, a gang of Dutch Nazi stormtroopers pushed their way into a Jewish ice cream parlor in South Amsterdam and viciously attacked the customers, who fought back. An uprising in a predominantly Jewish part of the old town followed. The German occupiers reacted with a manhunt; some four hundred young Jewish men were arrested and sent to Mauthausen, a much-dreaded concentration camp in Austria. Though they were nominally "hostages" held for potential exchange with German prisoners in enemy countries or for foreign payments, all but one of them would meet their deaths at the camp.

Amsterdammers countered the arrests with a huge general strike organized by the communist dock workers and other laborers. That defiant action entered Dutch history as the February Strike of 1941. The Nazi response was swift and intimidating, so the strike ended after two days. Yet, a statue known as *The Dock Worker* still stands in Amsterdam's former Jewish quarter in honor of the working men who showed solidarity with the beleaguered Jews of the Netherlands. Even now, each year on February 25, hundreds of people gather at the foot of the monument and leave flowers to commemorate the courageous strike of 1941. As anti-Semitic violence grew, more and more Dutch citizens dared to resist the occupation authorities.

In response to the street fighting, the Jewish quarters were temporarily sealed off, and three prominent Jewish leaders—representing the council of the main Dutch synagogue and the German-Jewish community (both Ashkenazi) as well as the Portuguese-Jewish (Sephardic) congregation—were summoned to a conference with occupation authorities. The latter demanded the immediate formation of a Jewish Council, to represent the Jews in the Netherlands and be responsible for their obedience to the occupiers' orders.

The council served as a mouthpiece for passing on German decrees. Its first duty was to order all Jews to surrender to the police "fire-arms, clubs, knives and other weapons" within twenty-four hours. If they did not comply, the Germans threatened to shoot five hundred Jews.[3]

Hitler had appointed fellow Austrian Dr. Arthur Seyss-Inquart to the lofty post of Reich Commissar.[4] His charge in the Netherlands was to assume all civilian functions and powers formerly exercised by the Dutch queen and her executive cabinet, who had fled the country just before its surrender to the German invaders. The Reich Commissar's office was located in The Hague's historic *Binnenhof* (Inner Court), the Dutch government buildings in the city center.

In reaction to the February strike, Reich Commissar Seyss-Inquart made a chilling speech. "We do not consider the Jews a part of the Dutch population," he said. "We will fight them wherever we meet them, and whosoever chooses their side will have to bear the consequences."[5]

Our friend Rudi Nussbaum was well aware of these ominous developments. He no longer slept at home, since roundups were often conducted at night. Yet, he continued going to school since he was close to getting his ship engineer diploma, which might come in good stead after the war. An artist and his wife who lived near the school put him up. His mother cooked dinner for him, and I biked over almost every day to take Rudi his main meal and spend a bit of time with him. At not yet fourteen, I was fascinated by the nineteen-year-old fellow, who had read much more than I and held opinions about people and events that were new to me.

Chapter Five

An Official at
the Reich Commissariat

✛ ✛ ✛

Early in 1941, Hans Calmeyer's story line and mine started
to converge. In December of 1940, he had interviewed for a
position with Dr. Carlo Stüler, the former district vice president of Osnabrück. Stüler held an appointment in the Office of
the Reich Commissar's Division of Interior Administration in
the Department of Justice and Interior Affairs, located in The
Hague. A cultured, widely read man, Stüler had joined the Nazi
Party without great conviction. He knew Calmeyer as a skilled
and resourceful lawyer and was well aware of the younger man's
anti-Hitler stance, but still saw Calmeyer as a welcome addition
to his hard-pressed staff.[1]

In January 1941, Reich Commissar Seyss-Inquart had
issued Decree 6/41, requiring all Jews in the Netherlands to register with their municipal offices. Article 4 defined who were to
be irrefutably considered Jews.

1. Jews are all persons whose grandparents included three
or more full Jews by race (see 3 below)

2. Persons with only two fully Jewish grandparents are deemed to be Jews if they either
   a. belonged to the Jewish religious community on May 9, 1940 (or subsequently joined it);
   b. or were married to a Jew on May 9, 1940, or after that date.

3. A grandparent is deemed a full Jew if (s)he was at any time a member of a Jewish religious congregation.[2]

German racial law was not consistent from the beginning, since the "racial" definition of a Jew was based on his or her grandparents' membership in a Jewish congregation. The implementation of this basically flawed law was different in Germany and in each of the Nazi-occupied countries—Austria, Czechoslovakia, Poland, Hungary, Denmark, Norway, Luxembourg, Belgium, and France. Moreover, rival factions within the Nazi Party and in the German bureaucracy competed to hold sway, resulting in a certain amount of arbitrariness and confusion.

Hans Calmeyer was charged with interpreting the registration law in the Netherlands and with settling any doubts as to whether a person was an Aryan, a full Jew, or a part Jew. In his new position, Calmeyer had considerable autonomy. Lives hung in the balance of his decisions. He soon found ways to use his legal skills in the service of his humane convictions.

In her 2009 study, Dutch lawyer Ruth van Galen-Herrmann underscores that Calmeyer immediately took exception to Article 3 of Decree 6/41, which said that a grandparent could be counted as irrefutably Jewish if he or she had been or was presently a member of the Jewish religious community.

Three weeks after he assumed his position at the Reich Commissariat, Calmeyer spoke up. Stüler, his immediate superior, asked him to detail his objections to the term "irrefutably" in a memorandum, and Calmeyer obliged on June 16, 1941. He argued that individuals should have the right to refute the assumption that a grandparent was racially Jewish if he or she was a member of a Jewish religious congregation. His reasoning was so persuasive that three days later, Reich Commissar Seyss-Inquart adopted Calmeyer's argument.[3]

Seyss-Inquart's decision gave Calmeyer the necessary discretion to allow petitioners to substantiate their contention with sworn testimonies or solemn declarations before Dutch administrative officials, who were usually cooperative. If a petitioner claimed that he or she was not and had never been a member of the Jewish community, a district court judge would summon the secretary of the congregation to refute that claim. Generally, the person summoned would not appear in court. Consequently, the petitioner's claim went unchallenged and hence was accepted by the judge.[4] The discretion Calmeyer created for his petitioners resulted in more than 5,600 cases of doubtful ancestry his office had to adjudicate.[5]

In addition, Calmeyer permitted petitioners to substantiate their requests with attestations by racial specialists of their own choosing, whereas in the German Reich, determinations in similar cases were based on findings by experts working for the Reich Office for Genealogical Research, the *Reichssippenamt*. Calmeyer's office also accepted testimonies from Jewish persons, which were not admissible within Germany.[6]

Calmeyer made another decision in favor of the petitioners in doubtful cases. In Germany the claimant had to prove without reasonable doubt that an unknown ancestor was an Aryan; in the Netherlands, Calmeyer's office had to establish whether the undocumented forebear was in fact Jewish.[7]

Equally helpful and of far-reaching consequence was Calmeyer's resolve to deal with the religion of children from mixed marriages according to Dutch law, which held that minors could not decide their religious affiliation. Hence, his office would not categorize the offspring of newly designated "mixed marriages" as J2, i.e., half-Jewish Jews, who would (eventually) have to wear the yellow star and be subject to deportation. Instead, children of these mixed marriages were routinely categorized as G1, of mixed blood and non-Jews, which meant they did not have to wear the star and would not be sent to a concentration camp.[8]

Requests to change a petitioner's registration came to Calmeyer's attention either via the RIB (*Rijksinspectie van de Bevolkingsregisters*), the country's superbly organized central registration office in The Hague, or directly from petitioners, most often via Dutch lawyers. Some of these Dutch colleagues tried to get closer to Calmeyer privately, but he politely turned down their invitations since private relationships with lawyers representing Jewish clients could awaken the mistrust of his compatriots.

Ostensibly, the Office for the Decision of Dubious Cases Regarding the Extraction According to Decree 6/41 sought to guarantee full rights to every pure-blooded Aryan; its covert purpose was to return as many Jews as possible to the general Dutch population. Those Aryanized by Calmeyer's office could resume previously forbidden positions and activities as if they had never been registered as Jews. This whittled down the count of Hitler's Jewish victims. Because of the way Decree 6/41 was written, there was no appeal to the decisions Calmeyer's office handed down.

Chapter Six

WEARING THE STAR OF DAVID

✣ ✣ ✣

June 11, 1941, brought another major roundup of Jewish young men. A German police official had requested that the Jewish Council provide a list of names of former students at an agricultural training facility to the north of Amsterdam. This was a teaching farm in the Wieringermeer *polder* (acres of fertile reclaimed land formerly below sea level), set up before the war to instruct young Jewish refugees in the principles of agriculture before the young men were to move on to Palestine, the area that is today Israel. The occupation authorities had closed the teaching farm. Now, the Jewish Council was told, the farm was to be reopened and the former students were to be officially contacted. Once the police had their addresses, however, all of the three hundred young men were arrested and sent to the Mauthausen annihilation camp. Among them was Rolf Schwarz, Rudi's best friend, who had joined our camping vacation.

A few weeks later, Rudi finished his final exam with flying colors. Bent on evading capture, he had the panniers of his bicycle packed, ready to leave Amsterdam the moment the exam was completed. He rode his bike again to Gelderland and, starting out from the home of the Jewish farmer where we had enjoyed our idyllic vacation the summer before, he found temporary shelter in several farmhouses in the area. Susi and I biked out there and celebrated my fourteenth birthday with Rudi. With the help of an artist friend, he had painted a pair of wooden shoes with several symbols and some verses. I was given the left shoe with my name on it, then sent on a treasure hunt to find the right one with his name to make it a pair. Clearly, Rudi was seeing me as his future partner. I was thrilled and flattered yet knew deep down that it would be premature to make life decisions at the age of fourteen.

Just three months after Rolf Schwarz's deportation to Mauthausen, we learned that Rudi's closest friend was dead. According to a preprinted postcard the SS camp administration sent to the families of all the young men of Rolf's transport, he had been shot while attempting to escape. Rudi was devastated and more determined than ever to stay out of the clutches of the German authorities.

It was not easy for him to find a place to hide for any length of time. Finally, a subsistence farmer and his family allowed Rudi to stay with them for an extended period. They had probably never seen a Jew before but simply felt that people needed to help each other.

Rudi told them, "I am Jewish. Anyone who helps a Jew may have to pay with his or her life. The man and his wife sat in their tiny living room and looked at each other. After they exchanged a few words, the man said to Rudi, "You can sleep in the hayloft, and where five people can eat their fill, there is also enough food for six."[1]

Happy to provide for their son's safety, Rudi's parents contributed a small monthly amount to the household expenses. He learned to till the soil, milk the cow, and cut timber alongside

Rudi's first hiding place, the little farm house in Vierhouten, picturesque but without running water or electricity

his "hiding father," Rik Teunissen. Soon a slightly more affluent neighboring farmer hired Rudi to help during planting and harvesting season so Rudi could make a little money.

To the neighbors, the people in the village of Vierhouten, Rudi was a city boy who needed fresh country air for health reasons. Occasionally, he would bike to the nearby town of Nunspeet to play the piano in the house of a Jewish family. At the Teunissens' he made do with his accordion, on which he entertained the family with Dvorak's "Slavonic Dances" and Smetana's "The Moldau." I visited Rudi several times during the year he stayed with them, and this hospitable family made me welcome as his girlfriend. We would ride our bicycles along narrow paths through heath and forests, Rudi ahead whistling a Beethoven or a Brahms melody, I following happily behind him. My main concern was that he would survive. Everything else, I trusted, would fall into place after the war, when I would be a little older.

Young sweethearts Rudi and Hansje near Vierhouten

Throughout the country, everyone over the age of fifteen
had to get an identity card. The cards for Jews bore a big fat
black "J" printed next to the owner's picture. Rudi collected his
identity card with the invidious J but soon managed to acquire
a false ID under a different name, without the telltale label. His
parents informed the Amsterdam registry office that their son
had moved away from home, new address unknown.

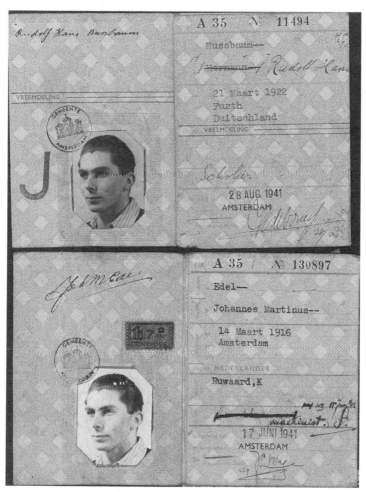

Rudi's real ID card and his forged one

At that point, everyone believed that only young Jewish
males were in danger. The rest of us simply had to adapt to the
encroachments on our freedom caused by increasingly restrictive
measures. My family and the Franks became closer as we coped
with wave after wave of anti-Jewish decrees.

In the fall of 1941, the German authorities announced that
Jewish students had to go to Jewish schools. Susi and I went to
an academic high school with a strong business program. Among
our electives were stenography, compound interest, and Spanish.
Margot and Anne Frank went to the Jewish Lyceum, where Greek
and Latin were offered as electives. We were all required to take
English, French, and German and quite a bit of algebra and geom-
etry, science, history, and geography. Our younger sister, Marli,
was a sixth grader at our neighborhood Jewish elementary school.

During most of the 1941–1942 school year, we could still
use public transportation. Our family lived at the edge of town.
Susi and I boarded the streetcar at its terminal, and Margot and
Anne and a dozen other Jewish secondary school students joined
us two stops later. Anne was always the center of a bevy of girls.

Our teachers were well qualified academically, but many
of them had no teaching experience. Several were from the
ranks of dismissed public servants. My math teacher had been a
pharmacist, my history teacher a curator and an art historian at
the *Rijksmuseum*. Thoughtless boys in my class gave her a hard
time, which upset me. I rebuked them for being so childish when
people already bore such heavy burdens.

In an effort to organize a private cultural life, many Jewish
families pooled their resources and played chamber music
together, invited singers and musicians to give in-house recitals,
and organized play readings.

I helped a group of younger teens mount a rendition of
The Princess with the Nose in our apartment under the aegis of

the refugee journalist who read the German classics with the older teenagers. I was the stage director, since I had brought the script from Frankfurt. My younger sister, Marli, and several of her friends performed, and Anne Frank played a leading role. I am no longer sure whether she was the queen or the princess, but I remember being struck by her vivaciousness. Yet, I did not take her quite seriously, since she was a little chatterbox.

Over the Christmas and Hanukkah holidays, Rudi visited his parents in Amsterdam for a few days. He went out only after nightfall when the streets were pitch dark because of the blackout, and he slept in the relatively safe apartment of my non-Jewish grandmother, Omi. As usual, we celebrated Christmas Eve at her place. Rudi brought two fountain pens, one for Susi and one for me. In his diary, he noted my enthusiasm and the happiness radiating from my eyes, which touched him.

In January 1942, SS General Reinhard Heydrich convened the infamous Wannsee Conference in a suburb of Berlin to discuss the "Final Solution to the Jewish Question." Fifteen high-level Nazi Party and government officials attended. Hitler had already authorized a policy of systematic physical annihilation. The purpose of the conference was to announce the decision to the higher echelons, to seek support for it, and to begin planning for its implementation throughout occupied Europe. None of the officials at the conference objected.

We were not aware of these policy decisions. For us, 1942 came with new Nazi decrees. Dutch Jews who did not live in

Amsterdam had to move there within three days, taking only what they could carry. Refugee Jews not living in Amsterdam would be moved to Camp Westerbork in the northeastern part of the country.

The three Klein sisters on their balcony. Left to right: Hansje, Marion, Susi

On the heels of the relocation ordinances came the decree that as of May 3, 1942, all Jews above the age of six had to wear a yellow Star of David whenever they left their home. The star, with the word *Jood* (Jew) printed on it in Hebrew-like characters, had to be sewn with small stitches onto the left front of outer garments. Stars were made of fabric and could be bought at the offices of the Jewish Council, at synagogues, and at a few other outlets for four cents apiece. One textile coupon had to be handed in for every four stars. Now, we were tarred and feathered!

Hansje's 9th grade class in the Jewish school. She is the fourth girl from the left.

I visited Rudi once more in late May 1942. Not wearing a star, I left our apartment in the early morning hours before our neighbors awoke and biked to the train station, where I felt reasonably safe due to my blue eyes and rather neutral features. But by the time summer vacation started, the situation for the Jews in Amsterdam had deteriorated so much that I no longer dared to take off my star and hop on the train.

The marginalization of the Jewish population was complete. Nonetheless, many non-Jews made a point of stopping in the street to express their empathy and concern, which was comforting. If they had listened surreptitiously to the BBC and heard some good news, they felt they could safely pass it on to a person wearing a star.

Even the BBC, however, had little good news in the summer of 1942. Although the United States had entered the war in December of 1941 and the German offensive in the Soviet Union had stalled, there was, as yet, no clear reversal.

Regarding the Jews under German rule, Adolf Eichmann, head of the Reich Security Office, Section IV B 4 in Berlin, sent an express letter to his counterpart at the Ministry of Foreign Affairs on June 22, 1942, in the same city. It confirmed plans for deportations, which began three weeks later.

SUBJECT: *Arbeitseinsatz* [Labor Mobilization] of Jews from France, Belgium and the Netherlands.

RE: Telephone call of 20.6.42 (June 20, 1942)

Arrangements have been made that from mid-July/the beginning of August of this year, Jews will be sent for labor in the Auschwitz camp, in special trains that will leave every day, which have room for 1,000 people—first of all about 40,000 Jews from the occupied French territory, 40,000 Jews from the Netherlands, and 10,000 Jews from Belgium. The people who are included are first of all Jews who are fit for labor, if they are not intermarried or hold the nationality of the British Empire, the USA, Mexico, enemy countries in Central or South America, or neutral or Allied countries.

I hope you will respond positively, and I assume that the Ministry of Foreign Affairs has no objection to these measures.

Upon order:
(signed) Eichmann [2]

Among the exceptions Eichmann noted were Jewish partners in a mixed marriage. They were protected Jews, and safe—for the moment, at least.

Chapter Seven

DIFFERENT DESTINIES

✥ ✥ ✥

The lives of the Franks and the Kleins took drastically different turns on July 5, 1942. On that fateful day, Margot Frank was among the first four thousand Jewish refugees, ages sixteen to forty, who received a summons to report within ten days for "labor" in Germany. My older sister, Susi, received the same order. Anne had just turned thirteen, my younger sister, Marli, was twelve, and I was almost fifteen, hence the three of us were too young to be called up. An itemized list specified what each person was allowed to take along: a backpack, a blanket, cutlery, metal dinnerware, and clothing, all of which made sense for a labor camp.

July 6, 1942, must have been our last day of school. Some sixteen-year-old refugee children who had lost a year in the transition from their German or Austrian schools to the Dutch education system were in my class. I remember the precise street corner where a little group of us stood and deliberated. It was at the foot of Amsterdam's one and only skyscraper, the capstone of the triangular Merwedeplein, where the Frank family lived.

One boy said, "Yes, I received a summons. My mother wants to hide me somewhere. I'll be darned if I'll allow myself to be cooped up for months or years to come. I'm strong, so working in a labor camp is fine with me."

A rather shy girl was in tears. "I, too, got the letter. I would much rather go into hiding," she sobbed, "but my parents won't hear of it. They're afraid that they and my baby sister and grandma will be rounded up if I don't appear at the appointed place with my backpack ready to go."

That same day, the Frank family disappeared. We did not inquire about their whereabouts. In those terrible years, it was better not to know anything that could be incriminating or harmful to others should we be forced to reveal it. A rumor circulated that they had escaped to Switzerland. During World War I, Otto Frank had served in the German Army, rising to the rank of lieutenant. We hoped that friends from the past had helped the family escape.

After the end of the war, we learned that the Franks had gone into hiding in secret quarters on the attic floor at the back of Mr. Frank's pectin business. The Van Pels family—Herman, Auguste, and son Peter (the Van Daans in the diary)—joined the Franks in their cramped quarters a few weeks later. Fritz Pfeffer (Dussel in the diary), a dentist who shared Anne's room (and commandeered her writing table to her chagrin), arrived in November 1942. Anne's famous diary vividly depicts the cloistered life of the eight people in the secret annex above the office and warehouse rooms, where regular work continued, directed by Otto through his partners. The Franks were able to hold out for twenty-five months, thanks to the loving care of Otto Frank's clerical staff and to the unwavering support of his business partners.

Hiding was not an easy option for those who had only recently arrived in the country. They did not have the network to connect them to helpful families or to the Dutch underground.

A few Jews who had valid visas for overseas countries could try to acquire a deferment in the hope that eventually they would be exchanged for German citizens living outside Europe. Others—Jewish doctors, pharmacists, teachers, even butchers and green grocers—could claim they were indispensable in serving the Jews of Amsterdam. Diamond workers, too, were still needed, as long as the German occupiers had use for their products. Not many refugees belonged in any of these categories.

One option open to refugee and Dutch Jews alike was claiming that they were wrongly categorized as Jews under Decree 6/41 and petitioning for a change in their registration status. It was Rudi's mother who first said to my parents, "If I had a non-Jewish mother, I would do my utmost to 'prove' that my father wasn't Jewish either in order to save myself and my family." Since my maternal grandmother was not Jewish, this was the escape route my family chose.

I don't remember when my parents first contacted a trustworthy Amsterdam lawyer about pursuing that option, but my mother's "Aryanization" case was already pending when my sister Susi received the summons to report for labor. Attorney Adriaan N. Kotting had already handed in a claim requesting the revision of my mother's registration as a Jew to Hans Calmeyer's office at the Reich Commissariat in The Hague.

In early 2015, Dr. Mathias Middelberg, a German lawyer and member of the current *Bundestag* (parliament), provided me with a copy of a document giving the date of my mother's original petition as May 7, 1942, which was four days after we had to start wearing the yellow star. Middelberg had written his doctoral dissertation on Hans Calmeyer's clever use of Nazi decrees to save thousands of Jews in the Netherlands.[1] Clearly my parents were aware of the dangers faced by all Jewish residents of the Netherlands months before the mass deportations began.

My maternal grandmother, Emma Blumenthal née Alscher, came from a highly musical Roman Catholic family in Austria. She and three of her sisters had formed a popular vocal close-harmony quartet, The Rohnsdorf Sisters, and toured the concert stages of Europe. As a young singer, she'd had a passionate love affair with a Jewish businessman, Berthold Blumenthal. Soon, she was expecting a child. The lovers wanted to get married in 1898, but Mr. Blumenthal's mother was strictly against her son marrying a non-Jewish woman. My grandparents postponed their wedding until after my great-grandmother's death. Their daughter Marianne ("Mia")—my mother—was twenty years old when her parents finally got married. Her father's filial deference to his mother's wishes eventually saved my family's lives.

The "Rohnsdorf Sisters," early to mid-1890s. The author's grandmother, Emma, is the first one on the left.

From 1919 on, my mother was Marianne Blumenthal, but she had previously gone by Maria Anna Felicitas Alscher. From when she was six until she was thirteen, little Mia had lived in Dresden in the home of a Protestant foster family while my grandmother pursued her singing career all over Europe. Summer breaks Mia would spent vacationing with her parents. In 1913, my grandmother gave up her singing career, retrieved her daughter, and set up house in Vienna, where my mother received her secondary education. Her childhood had not been an easy one, but it was now potentially our salvation.

Emma Alscher (Rohnsdorf) with little Mia around 1906

In 1942, my mother's beloved biological Jewish father had already been dead for fourteen years. Mr. Kotting, their good lawyer, helped my parents come up with the necessary Aryan father and with a story that stood a chance of passing Hans Calmeyer's legal inspection. Kotting suggested that my mother declare that her Protestant foster father, Max Hentzschel, also long dead, had sired her. Mr. Hentzschel's widow refused to perjure herself, but my maternal grandmother and her younger sister swore the necessary oaths. Moreover, there were my mother's Dresden school report cards from the years 1906–1913, countersigned by Max Hentzschel, and in addition, some family photos in which my mother looked enough like her foster brothers to be taken for their half-sister.

Thus, my mother was able to claim that she was not really half-Jewish, since Berthold Blumenthal had entered her life twenty years after her birth, when he married her mother. Only then, in 1919, had he declared Marianne Alscher his daughter and given her his name, a generous gesture that needed to be undone. The contention was a falsehood based on some truths. We desperately hoped it would serve its lifesaving purpose.

Chapter Eight

Roundups

✣ ✣ ✣

Since many of the people summoned to report for labor failed to show up at the appointed place and time, the German authorities soon resorted to arbitrary roundups in parts of Amsterdam heavily populated by Jews. They barged in and took whole families, including babies and grandmothers, to fill the quota of deportations that had been established by Himmler in Berlin. Even the most optimistic people began to realize that something much more sinister than sending Jews to "labor camps" was taking place.

In *The Dutch Under German Occupation*, Werner Warmbrunn quoted from the September 1942 issue of the underground newspaper *Verzet* (Resistance):

> In the quiet streets of the *Zuid* [the southern part of Amsterdam] you hear suddenly the noise of many cars, the hated Green Police vans in which the Germans fetch their victims. . . . They descend from the vans . . . the Green Police and their Dutch henchmen.
>
> In a short time . . . it begins: on each corner stand German agents, rifles slung across their shoulders. . . .

They noisily climb upstairs: "Are any Jews living here?"
And then the Jews of Holland are driven together on
the street corner. Men and women and children . . .
stand on the corner of their own street, alone and
abandoned. No, thank God, not abandoned, there
are Christians, real Christians, human beings with
a heart in their breasts who come to their aid. Look,
they reason with the uniformed Germans, they plead
with them, and persist even when threatened that
they, too, will be taken along. They bring food and
candy and warm clothes to the unfortunate Jews,
and then they run off to tell relatives who live in the
neighborhood what is happening to their families. . . .

From the fourth floor a Jew leaps to his death
rather than fall into the hands of the Germans. The
Germans followed him up to the roof after they had
searched closets and cellars, attics and tool sheds. A
dog who defends his master . . . is shot down by the
Germans. That is the only shot fired that night. . . .

Everybody walking through the neighborhood
is stopped at each corner and has to show his identity
card. If he has the fatal "J" on his card, he is lost. If
not, he can walk on, until another policeman has to
be satisfied at the next corner. . . .

Then comes the end. The big green vans start their
engines and begin to move. The engines keep roaring
till a quarter to twelve. . . . The vans bring their load
to the Gestapo Building, to the *Joodse Schouwburg*
[former Jewish Theater] and elsewhere.

And then the transports start leaving the city.[1]

On August 6, 1942, my mother, sisters, and I were among two thousand Jews hauled out of our apartments and taken to the *Zentralstelle für jüdische Auswanderung*, the Central Office for Jewish Emigration at the Adama van Scheltema Square.

It was a sunny day. People milled around in what was once a schoolyard. My mother had brought her papers. After several hours, she was permitted to present them to someone in authority, who found her name on Hans Calmeyer's list of pending cases. We were allowed to go just as my feisty grandmother came marching in to give the person in charge an earful. Luckily my father had not been home when we were apprehended. With our case still undecided, he might not have been let go. My parents urged our lawyer to do his utmost to push for a quick and favorable decision in The Hague. Mr. Kotting retorted that there were many petitioners and that we had to wait our turn.

With deportations in full swing in 1942, more people who had registered as Jews were reviewing their ancestry and claiming Aryan forebears. As Hans Calmeyer developed and refined his office procedures, he needed more staff, people who shared his views but could be trusted to maintain a façade of loyalty to Hitler and adherence to German law. Any staff member with anti-Nazi feelings too strong to mask would endanger the rescue operation as a whole.

Calmeyer was extremely lucky with Heinrich Miessen, who joined his office in February of 1942. A World War I invalid with a perpetually stiff leg, Miessen walked with difficulty, aided by a cane with a silver knob. An early pensioner and a hobby genealogist, he was particularly knowledgeable in the border region of the German Rhineland, the Netherlands, and Belgium.

Miessen arrived at Calmeyer's office with his own portable typewriter. His lapel was decorated with a Nazi Party badge and insignia that identified him as a local officer and ideological trainer of the Nazi Party. The new employee was struck that Calmeyer wore no badges and did not display a picture of Hitler on any of his office walls. At the beginning, each man expected the other to be a staunch, probably fanatical follower of the Führer. During their interview, they somehow divined each other's true inclinations. Calmeyer came to understand that Miessen's badges were mere camouflage and that Miessen was as scandalized by the Nazis' persecution of Jews as he was.[2]

A second fortunate, like-minded hire was Dr. Gerhard Wander, a lawyer from East Prussia, whom Calmeyer requested from another office at the Reich Commissariat. Wander joined Calmeyer's team in October 1942. He had a Jewish girlfriend, and he was in contact with the Dutch as well as the German underground.[3]

An unwelcome addition to Calmeyer's office in 1942 was the zealous Dutch SS Corporal Ludo ten Cate, who had genealogical expertise gathered in the Netherlands specifically concerning its South American, "West Indian," colonies. Thanks to financial support from Dutch Nazi circles, he had at his disposal piles of dossiers and over 300,000 file cards bearing genealogical information. Eventually Ten Cate headed the Dutch Central Service for Genealogy and was authorized to receive copies of Calmeyer's decisions, which he scrutinized. From time to time, Ten Cate exposed substantiating "evidence" that was either forged or fictitious, and more than once he denounced Calmeyer to SS General Hanns Albin Rauter, the head of the Dutch and German police and a close associate of Reich SS leader, Heinrich Himmler. In such cases Calmeyer coolly played down the discrepancies and called Ten Cate a hothead.[4]

Nonetheless, Ten Cate posed a great risk to Calmeyer's endeavors. Louis de Jong, the authoritative Dutch historian of the occupation years, deemed him Calmeyer's most dangerous antagonist. Eventually Ten Cate left the scene, when he was ordered to join the military, but that was not until August 1944.[5]

In the midst of Reich Commissar Dr. Seyss-Inquart's headquarters in The Hague, with no interference from Carlo Stüler, Calmeyer's immediate superior, it was possible for Calmeyer, Miessen, Wander, and their staff to sabotage the racial laws for a while. Their strategy was to protect Jews designated for deportation and eventual slaughter through a time-consuming bureaucratic system based on "thorough investigations" and "official findings." They seized every opportunity to delay negative decisions, and steadfastly refused attempts at bribery. When one petitioner put a bagful of rough diamonds on Miessen's desk, he was told, "You'd better take those pebbles home again. They won't do you any good here."[6]

Early in the occupation, numerous clever people learned to craft falsified identity cards. They extended their skills to forge realistic-looking baptismal certificates, school, and marriage records, archival documents authenticated by expertly fabricated rubber stamps. Calmeyer was inclined to accept statements based largely on oaths or on probably forged but legally appropriate documents. Critical experts have judged that as many as 95 percent of the documents presented to Calmeyer and his staff were counterfeit. On the other hand, appeals based on sentiment or tearful, person-to-person pleas did not sway his judgment, which was always disciplined and based on the letter of the law.

Only if a case might draw attention from Nazi officials less inclined to leniency did Calmeyer reject evidence presented on behalf of a Jewish petitioner. Some claims were so obviously bogus that he had to turn them down. Even then, he helped as best he could. Calmeyer's office would forewarn petitioners whose cases were to be rejected, giving them a chance to go into hiding before Nazi police could come for them.[7] In all his remaining years, Calmeyer agonized over how little he had been able to do to save the Jews of the Netherlands from wholesale slaughter.

By the autumn of 1942, while my mother's case was still pending, the suspicions of several high-ranking Nazis were roused by the increasing number of Jews deferred from deportation, and the high proportion of favorable decisions issuing from Calmeyer's office. Within the Reich Commissar's headquarters, one heard a number of neologisms. "Calmeyer Jews" were those granted deferrals because their descent was still being investigated, and the verb "to Calmeyer" meant to change a person's official status from having to register as a Jew to being recognized as half-Jewish, one quarter Jewish, or not Jewish at all. Calmeyer and his cohorts banked on the premise that even the staunchest anti-Semites wanted to keep up a semblance of lawfulness.

Among Calmeyer's early adversaries was Adolf Eichmann's close associate Dr. Erich Rajakowitsch, the SS officer in charge of the "Special Section, Jewish Affairs" in the Netherlands (a subdivision of the SS Main Office for the Security of the Reich in Berlin). Rajakowitsch's successor, Wilhelm Zoepf, became a still more outspoken enemy. Together with other Nazi officials, Zoepf suspected Calmeyer of fraud and began to demand case-by-case reviews of his approvals. As the days went by, our family's fate grew ever more precarious.

The "Calmeyer list," the deferment list of as yet unresolved cases, appeared in print for the first time on September 8, 1942. It bore the names of over 1,500 petitioners, including my mother's. Later that fall, the original list was supplemented by dozens more names of people whose petitions for genealogical review had yet to be acted upon.[8] These persons were therefore exempt from having to report for labor in the East, hence from deportation. A deferment stamp on their identity cards confirmed their status. Nonetheless, some people with the coveted stamp were sent to Camp Westerbork near the German border and held there until Calmeyer's office rendered a decision.

The SD (*Sicherheitsdienst*, the Nazi Intelligence Service) grew tired of Calmeyer's deferment lists. On November 25, 1942, the Commissioner General for Special Duties, Fritz Schmidt, addressed a note to "Party Member Dr. Callmeyer." Calmeyer was not a party member, he did not have a doctor's title, and his name was spelled with a single "l." The message was a slap in the face. The SD wanted Calmeyer to stop submitting ever more lists of Jews claiming they were Aryans. Therefore, according to Schmidt, Reich Commissar Seyss-Inquart had decided no more lists were to be handed in after December 1 of the current year. Dubious cases were henceforth to be submitted to Seyss-Inquart himself.

Calmeyer took Schmidt's note directly to Seyss-Inquart. The Reich Commissar read it and said, "Oh, dear colleague, just continue your work. What would otherwise become of our Jews?"[9] Within a few weeks, however, under pressure from the SD/SS, Seyss-Inquart told Calmeyer he had better wind down his activities. Calmeyer disregarded the directive and carried on with his reclassifications, albeit with heightened circumspection.

Chapter Nine

SABOTAGING HITLER'S
FINAL SOLUTION

✢ ✢ ✢

By the fall of 1942, Rudi no longer felt safe in the rural surroundings of Vierhouten. There was a new Nazi mayor, and the police
had found and arrested some Jews hiding literally underground
in the forest. Rudi got in touch with the Dutch resistance, who
provided him with a hiding place on the outskirts of Amsterdam
with Mr. and Mrs. Arie Blokland. On his way there, he saw his
parents once again and pleaded with them to pack up and disappear. Rudi found his parents a hiding address, but when trusted
people came to take them to safety, his parents had already been
seized and sent to Camp Westerbork, which functioned as a
holding tank for Jews awaiting further deportation.

When the 1942–1943 school year started, my sisters and
I had to walk forty-five minutes each way to and from school.
Jews had been ordered to hand in their bicycles and were no
longer allowed to use public transportation as of early summer
1942. Our classes had drastically shrunk; every day fewer students showed up. We learned not to ask whether they had been

deported or gone into hiding, but rather to put on blinders and try to concentrate on French irregular verbs and chemistry formulas. Before the first semester was over, my class of tenth-graders was reduced to a group of five or six.

Soon, Susi found herself the only remaining student in eleventh grade, the highest level in our type of secondary school. She was completely dispirited. I remember our chemistry teacher taking me aside and urging me to encourage my sister not to give up. Our teachers knew, of course, that sooner rather than later their deferments would be annulled. As soon as there were no more students left, our educators and their families would find themselves on the next transport unless they had secured a hiding place.

With Rudi's parents and practically all our Jewish friends and neighbors gone, it was hard not to be discouraged. Yet my family always believed that our petition was quite convincing, and our lawyer assured us that a favorable decision could be expected before long.

Day after day, Hans Calmeyer and his coworkers had to make life-or-death determinations. I surmise that they agonized about the fact that whatever they ruled, they were complicit, for they participated in a murderous administrative system. If they resigned from their positions, they risked being succeeded by doctrinaire Nazis and anti-Semites, who would cancel whatever successes they had achieved. In internal office discussions, they probably encouraged each other to persist in their rescue operation despite growing antagonism. They must have reasoned that even if their challengers detected false documents, they could not prove that Calmeyer and his staff had been aware of the forgeries and had wittingly allowed themselves to be deceived.

In a lighter vein, Heinrich Miessen, utterly familiar with the thinking of the Nazis, once sent the Reich Office for Genealogy a forceful complaint alleging that others in the administration looked down on the office for which he worked as "superfluous and not essential to the war effort." They did so, he continued tongue in cheek, despite the fact that it was "general knowledge by now, that this war is in final analysis a racial war."[1]

Intense rivalry persisted about who was in charge of matters concerning the Jews in the Netherlands. On the one hand was Reich Commissar Seyss-Inquart, the highest German civilian authority in The Hague, and on the other were the powerful SS and SD offices in Amsterdam. As early as 1941, the highest-ranking SS and SD security officers in Berlin, Adolf Eichmann and Reinhard Heydrich, tried to make the persecution and deportation of the Jews their exclusive domain. Reich Commissar Seyss-Inquart would have none of this, but he was not authoritative enough to prevail unequivocally. A confusing situation of conflicting jurisdictions remained. Over the years, the power shifted gradually toward the SS and SD. Rajakowitsch, who worked for the SD, was eager to secure for his service the right to make decisions in cases of dubious extraction. He got his way, but only insofar as direct dealings with German offices were concerned, for instance, in confiscation cases.

A major challenge came from Hanns Albin Rauter, an esteemed "old fighter," as those who had joined the Nazi Party before it came to power were called, and a close associate of Reich SS leader Heinrich Himmler. Rauter, commissioner general for security, was in control of the Security Service as well as of the Dutch and German police in the Netherlands. In a secret letter to his colleague Dr. Friedrich Wimmer, who was in charge of Internal Affairs and Justice (the official to whom Stüler reported), Rauter expressed his interest in having his man, SS Brigade Commander Dr. Wilhelm Harster, participate in decisions about doubtful cases.

Luckily, Calmeyer was able to turn Ludo ten Cate's link with his office to advantage. He responded obligingly to the demand by declaring it was his "intention that the head of the Dutch Central Office for Genealogy [would] have jurisdiction."[2] Because Ten Cate was a Dutch member of the SS, the German SS leaders considered him a reliable follower of the party line and let the matter drop for the moment.

From time to time, Calmeyer had visitors from his home city. Gottfried Woldering was the son of an Osnabrück family that belonged to one of the anti-Nazi circles Calmeyer and his wife had frequented before the war. He paid three visits to Calmeyer in The Hague. During the first one he noticed how much Calmeyer had changed. Once an upbeat freethinker and a bon-vivant, he had become serious, pensive, circumspect, and reserved. When Woldering asked his friend what he was actually doing in the occupied country, Calmeyer replied that he was working for the Interior Department, in charge of a kind of citizens' registry.

Only during a later visit in mid-1944 did Calmeyer tell the young man that he was the head of the "Office for the Decision of Dubious Cases Regarding the Extraction according to Decree 6/41." He said that he was attempting to help endangered people. "You see, I am trying to prevent even more trains from leaving from Vught," he explained.[3] In Vught in the Dutch province of Brabant, a transit camp for Jews and a concentration camp for political prisoners was established in 1942. Both Woldering and Calmeyer knew that most trains from Vught went to Westerbork, and that from there thousands of Jews were deported either to forced-labor camps, where "natural reduction" in numbers occurred, or to extermination camps such as Treblinka. Both had also had experiences with Dutch Nazis and considered them even worse than their German counterparts.

Woldering confided that he was in touch with the Dutch resistance. Calmeyer advised him to proceed with caution and restraint. "We do not need heroes!" he said emphatically. "What we need is small-scale resistance."[4]

My family received the lifesaving decision on our Aryanization petition from the Reich Commissariat on January 21, 1943. It was printed on official stationery, with the German eagle atop a swastika. According to the text, my mother was no longer required to register as a Jew, and my sisters and I were henceforth regarded as being of mixed blood. My father was to be considered a partner in a "privileged mixed marriage." The document was signed by Dr. Gerhard Wander. That very night my mother, my sisters, and I unstitched the stars from our garments, shedding them with happy sighs of relief!

Through my 2015 correspondence with Dr. Mathias Middelberg, the German lawyer and politician who had written his doctoral dissertation about Calmeyer's finessing of the "Jewish laws" in the Netherlands, I learned something new: the all-important letter Dr. Gerhard Wander had signed on January 21, 1943, was not the official document we had so anxiously been waiting for. Middelberg sent me a copy of Calmeyer's actual decision signed on March 9, 1943. I was struck by Calmeyer's carefully worded argumentation as to why my mother should not be considered half-Jewish, based on the papers her Dutch lawyer had submitted pertaining to her illegitimate birth to a non-Jewish mother.

What I read in Calmeyer's report on our case was that as early as March 26, 1942, the Dutch District Court in Amsterdam had established that my mother was not the natural child of Berthold Blumenthal, and on July 16, 1942, that same court had satisfied itself that neither my mother nor my sisters and I had been members of a Jewish congregation on the day of the Dutch

DER REICHSKOMMISSAR
FÜR DIE BESETZTEN NIEDERLÄNDISCHEN GEBIETE

DER GENERALKOMMISSAR
FÜR VERWALTUNG UND JUSTIZ

HAUPTABTEILUNG INNERES

Entscheidungsstelle
über die Meldepflicht aus VO 6/41

Dr.W.TS

DEN HAAG,   den 21 Januar 1943
Scheveningscheweg 17
Tel. 117760

An die Herren Rechtsanwälte Dr.H.v.Krimpen
Mr.H.B.Wieringa & Mr.A.N.Kotting

A M S T E R D A M
Vondelstraat 30

In dem Abstammungsverfahren Klein-Alscher
ist durch Beschluss vom heutigen Tage folgende
Entscheidung getroffen:

1. Maria Anna Felicitas Klein, geb. Alscher
wird im Sinne der VO 6/41 als nicht melde-
pflichtig erklärt.

2. Suzanna Charlotte Klein
Hannelore Alice Klein
Maria Alice Klein
werden unter Abänderung der bisherigen
Registrierung als Mischling I.Grades eingeordnet

3. die Ehe der Edmund Josef Klein und Maria
Anna Felicitas Alscher, wird als privile-
gierte Mischehe festgestellt.

(Dr.Wander)

The all-important Aryanization document, dated January 21, 1943 capitulation. Whether or not our mother's foster father, Max Hentzschel, had sired her, was under the given circumstances of no importance, Calmeyer declared. The fact that the petitioner was born out of wedlock to an Aryan mother justified the presumption that her procreator was Aryan as well. There were no indications suggesting that she was sired by a Jew. Consequently, the petitioner was not subject to registration, and her three children were to be re-categorized as of mixed blood, grade I. Her marriage to our Jewish father was to be considered a privileged mixed marriage.

Calmeyer had not used the official stationery of the Reich Commissariat, with the eagle and the swastika, but ordinary blank typewriter paper, because the three-page document was meant for internal use only, in case he was called upon to justify his determination.

We now know that Dr. Wander had not been authorized to sign off on decisions. Eager to act, he had jumped the gun in our case, as well as in others. Eventually, Calmeyer dismissed him. There were probably several reasons, among them fear that Wander's want of caution would endanger the thoughtful rescue operation of the entire Office for the Decision of Dubious Cases Regarding the Extraction According to Decree 6/41.[5]

For my family, however, Wander's premature letter of January 21, 1943, came none too soon. All five of us were out of danger, and after shedding our stars, my mother, my sisters, and I could again participate in normal life, insofar as there was such a thing three years into the war. Mother was again able to buy our food at any time the stores were open, and we three girls could go back to regular schools. Susi finished her last high school year in the school where she and I had started our secondary education. For her it was especially important that she had a few months of regular school before the final national matriculation exam. I opted for the

Girls' Lyceum, partly because I was sick and tired of the childish fifteen-year-old boys I had gone to school with and partly because the Girls' Lyceum was Margot Frank's original school. She had long been my model. Our youngest sister, Marli, joined me there.

When I entered my new tenth-grade class in the middle of the school year, I was accepted without any questions asked. There were other half-Jewish students, so that was no problem. The few Nazi girls in our class were barely tolerated, hence they kept very quiet.

Just before summer vacation, the upper grades of my school went on a three-day field trip. We slept in bunk beds three levels high, similar to the beds in the Westerbork barracks, as we had learned from the short notes that had reached us from there. I remember the heartache, thinking of my Jewish friends who were relegated to bunk beds, not for a cheerful vacation break but under dire, unhygienic, and primitive circumstances, in daily fear for their lives. I did not know at the time that most of them were already dead.

Most important to me, after shedding our stars, was the fact that I could now again move about freely and bike to where Rudi was hiding. I could take him books to keep his mind occupied and be of help to him in many small ways. Rudi's parents were still in the transit camp Westerbork on Dutch soil. His father was serving as a pharmacist in the camp infirmary. For as long as that lasted, both he and his wife would be deferred from deportation. Nobody knew exactly what happened to the tens of thousands of people shipped in cattle cars from Westerbork to undisclosed destinations. Since those sent east were never heard from again, people feared the worst and tried to postpone their own departure as long as possible.

The Nussbaums could receive packages at Westerbork. They had stored some supplies and clothing with friendly neighbors and particularly needed soap, food, warm sweaters, and rain gear. Now I could get to their belongings. My mother packed them in parcels, which Susi and I took to the post office on our bikes. Mother also made packages for many other friends and neighbors who were still at Westerbork. Being so closely tied to their fate, we felt that this was the least we could do.

Under the date March 27, 1943, Anne Frank, hiding with her family and four others in the attic she called the "back quarters," noted in her diary: "Rauter, one of the German big shots, has made a speech: 'All Jews must be out of the German-occupied countries before July 1. Between April 1 and May 1, the province of Utrecht must be cleaned out [as if the Jews were cockroaches]. Between May 1 and June 1, the provinces of North and South Holland.' These wretched people are sent to filthy slaughterhouses like a herd of sick, neglected cattle."[6]

Indeed, during the spring and summer of 1943, deportations of Jews continued steadily. Deferments were annulled one after another. By September 29 of that year, even the highest leaders of the Jewish Council, the diamond magnate Abraham Asscher and David Cohen, a professor of ancient history, were arrested and taken to Westerbork. The Netherlands had been "cleaned out" except for Jews in mixed marriages, the Portuguese Jews, people on Calmeyer's list, and some 20,000–25,000 Jews in hiding.[7]

The status of the roughly four thousand Portuguese Jews was as yet undecided. In the early sixteenth century, their Sephardic forefathers had converted to Catholicism under coercion of the Spanish Crown and the Inquisition. Calmeyer voiced the opinion that by the 1940s, bloodlines had been so diluted that "pure"

Portuguese Jews no longer existed. He instituted a special list for Portuguese petitioners and supported their lawyers' considerable endeavors to save large numbers of Portuguese Jews from deportation by assembling elaborate family trees. All of these efforts eventually failed. In early 1944, a review foisted upon Calmeyer by SS officer Wilhelm Zoepf and race experts in Berlin came to the conclusion that the Portuguese petitioners were "racially subhuman beings" and should be treated like other Jews. They were rounded up and sent first to Westerbork, then to *Theresienstadt* (Terezin), and ultimately to their deaths in Auschwitz.[8]

Chapter Ten

THE TIDE IS TURNING

✤ ✤ ✤

By the spring of 1943, the German Army had surrendered near Stalingrad, and Allied troops had launched successful offensives in North Africa. In the Netherlands, the Germans were still in control, but the once cocksure occupiers lost some of their self-confidence and also some of their opportunistic Dutch followers. A tide of resistance rose all over the country. Dutch physicians refused en masse to allow themselves to be organized in a German-style professional association. They did so in such a well-disciplined fashion that the occupation authorities had to give in.

The Dutch university students were not quite as successful in their refusal to sign a loyalty declaration designed by the Reich Commissariat in cooperation with the Dutch National Socialist Party (NSB). Yet the percentage of students who signed was nowhere higher than 25 percent, and three Dutch universities chose to close down.

Another major event in March 1943 was a carefully planned assault on the Amsterdam Central Registry of the Population. The aim was to destroy as many registration cards as possible and to do so without bloodshed. For the Jews of Amsterdam, the destruction of the registry came too late. However, lacunae in the records made it easier for the underground to issue falsified identity cards that could not be checked against an official Amsterdam record.

The second major strike in the Netherlands began on April 19, 1943. It was triggered by a decree issued by the German Military Commander for the occupied country, Air Force General Friedrich Christiansen: all Dutch soldiers who had been taken prisoner of war and who were released after the capitulation of the Dutch Army in 1940 were to be interned and sent to Germany to work for the war effort. By the end of April, many tens of thousands of Dutch people were on strike. The occupation authorities had not expected this widespread reaction. Fearing the strike might spill over to Belgium and France, they reacted with mass arrests and sent in troops with live ammunition, causing 140 deaths.[1]

Acute manpower shortage led the occupiers to recruit ever more Dutchmen for their factories. Few volunteered, so forced labor was instituted for all men who did not already support the war effort or could not prove they were indispensable in their present jobs. Many eligible men went underground, which helped Jews in as much as hiding became a way of life in the Netherlands, and falsified identity papers and ration cards were more easily obtainable. On the other hand, the number of safe hiding places was limited in the small and transparent country, where dense population, flat terrain, and lack of wilderness made it hard to conceal illicit activities. Families who might have taken in endangered Jews now had nephews, cousins, and other kinsfolk to hide.

Tensions between the SS/SD and the Office for the Decision of Dubious Cases grew acute. In May 1943, the SD demanded that the list of Calmeyer Jews be reexamined case by case, since many were of such a "pronounced Galician physiognomy" as to cast doubt on the accuracy of Calmeyer's genealogical review. The ever-growing lists, they charged, were a ploy to stall for time.

Moreover, the SS/SD no longer wanted to respect "privileged mixed marriages," in which a Jew and a non-Jew had married and produced children. Previously, the Jewish partner in such marriages had been exempted from deportation. But in the spring of 1943, the SD gave Jewish men in mixed marriages the choice between deportation or sterilization. Zoepf reasoned that extending any kind of privileges to the almost 18,800 Jewish partners in mixed marriages in the Netherlands would "seriously endanger the general dejudification."

Using strictly legalistic arguments and citing different rules prevailing in Germany, Calmeyer registered protest in several official meetings. In the end, the churches objected to the sterilization program, and the measure was abandoned.[2] Yet, many Jewish men in mixed marriages were forced to work as day laborers.

When my father was called up to do day labor for the occupying forces, a chest X-ray revealed an ominous tuberculosis scar, dating back to World War I. For fear of contamination, my father was excused from forced labor. Here was another case of early misfortune that turned into a blessing.

As attacks on the work of his office became frequent and pointed, Calmeyer and his colleagues had to turn down petitioners when corroborating evidence was too weak to withstand hostile scrutiny. This furnished the grounds on which a Dutch lawyer, Mrs. L. M. I. L. van Taalingen-Dols, would testify against Calmeyer after the war, claiming that he could—and hence should—have saved more Jewish lives.[3]

In 1943, Calmeyer broke his own rule against allowing

personal sympathies to influence decisions when Henny Hirsch, his former Jewish secretary, unexpectedly appealed to him for help. She was married to a Jewish man named Heinz Koppel, and she was pregnant. After approaching his adversary Zoepf, and possibly also Seyss-Inquart, who tended to be open to special cases, Calmeyer was granted a free hand. The Koppels were deported to Bergen-Belsen, at the time the preferential camp for Jews who might be exchanged for German prisoners or nationals abroad. Through Swedish intervention, the Koppels were subsequently sent to Switzerland and eventually reached the Promised Land, the future Israel but at that time still Palestine.[4]

With several people in Westerbork eagerly awaiting Calmeyer's decision as to their racial reclassification, his clerk, a young Dutch lawyer named Jacob van Proosdij, took over assignments at the transit camp, helping to shield people while their cases were pending. Mathias Middelberg cites the case of well-known Berlin actress Camilla Spira. After Calmeyer's office had decided her petition favorably, Spira was allowed to return from Westerbork to Amsterdam.[5]

Besides protecting people at Westerbork while the decisions on their petitions were still pending, Van Proosdij purloined rubber stamps, stationery, and envelopes from the Reich Commissariat, which his activist Dutch colleagues used to falsify letters and documents. He always had the latest inside information regarding genealogical decisions, which he passed on to his fellow lawyers, foremost at the law office of Kotting and associates, where Van Proosdij had worked before joining Calmeyer's staff.[6]

Adjudication of reclassification requests continued. Heinrich Miessen listened as he usually did to what his heart told him. In the case of a certain Alexander Lifschütz, Miessen had received an unambiguous report from Bremen: there was no doubt that the man was of fully Jewish descent. Miessen destroyed these documents and claimed that the combination of the petitioner's given names (Alexander Joseph Berthold) did not occur in any Jewish family. He had based this contention, he said, on many years of genealogical research. The petition was approved.[7]

In Middelberg's account of the case, Lifschütz had not filled in the slots pertaining to his grandparents. Calmeyer noted in his decision that it would have fallen to his office to prove that the petitioner's grandparents were Jewish.[8]

Chapter Eleven

BOLTING OUT OF REACH

✛ ✛ ✛

The inmates at camp Westerbork were severely limited in the number and length of postcards they could send out. Rudi's mother, Ella, managed to pass messages to my parents via helpful couriers. They had special permits allowing them to travel back and forth between Westerbork and Amsterdam to help supply the camp with basic necessities. In August of 1943, Ella herself got permission to travel to Amsterdam for two days to procure medical supplies for the camp pharmacy. She and Rudi secretly saw each other one last time, a most dramatic reunion.

Taking in her beloved son's pale and toneless face after ten months of hiding inside a small duplex, Ella urged Rudi to turn himself in and go with her to Westerbork. Young people there played soccer and engaged in other outdoor activities after work. Rudi knew better. He was sorely tempted to plead with his mother to go into hiding then and there, but if Ella Nussbaum did not return to Westerbork, Hermann, her husband, would be sent east on the next transport.

When I saw Rudi a few days later, he was visibly shaken from the wrenching experience. He was getting more and more stir crazy

Rudi's mother, Ella Nussbaum, in Bellinzona, Switzerland, late 1930s

and prevailed upon his activist "hiding father," Arie Blokland, to put him in touch with the Dutch underground. After several weeks of waiting, he learned there was a possibility of traveling through Belgium and France to the Spanish border, ostensibly in service of the German war effort. Luckily his parents had given him some small gold coins for emergency use. He sold one to acquire a set of superbly falsified papers that said that he, Mr. Johannes Martinus Edel, was charged with the purchase of technical equipment for the German Navy, and that he was to be given all possible assistance.

Rudi's forged special paper, documenting him, Johannes M. Edel, as a Dutch agent

As a trial run, Rudi had to travel to The Hague to meet with a liaison. With his bright blue eyes and his dark hair bleached to a fiery Irish red, he came out of hiding and passed the checkpoints at the stations of Amsterdam and The Hague, saluting with a nonchalant, *"Heil Hitler."*

Rudi did extremely well at the meeting. A week later, he boarded a special train for German soldiers, the SS, and the occupiers' civil servants and made his way via Maastricht (in the southeast of the Netherlands) and Paris to the foot of the Pyrenees, the mountain range that separates France from Spain. The Dutch underground had given him a contact address in Tarbes, where he was to link up with a trustworthy member of the French resistance. That person would find him a reliable guide for crossing the heavily guarded border region.

Sadly, there had been some recent cases of betrayal, and the link to the *maquis,* the French resistance, was broken. Trying to cross the Pyrenees on his own would have been foolhardy. Rudi's school French was a far cry from the regional dialect. The border region was teeming with spies and traitors. He would have been recognized as a stranger and taken to the German authorities for a bounty, and that would have been the end. Rudi's French was, however, good enough to locate a typewriter in Tarbes, and he created a new set of travel papers for the journey back to Amsterdam.

In his eagerness to return, he decided to take the direct route from Paris via Brussels rather than the more easterly detour via Maastricht, which he'd used on his way south. That turned out to be a serious mistake. Later he shared his ordeal in an interview:

> When I came to the Belgian-Dutch border, I was made to leave the train and taken to the border police at the station. I tried to impress the officer on duty by voicing loud indignation. What were they thinking, taking me off the train, when I had an all-important meeting the next day in Hamburg, where the navy needed crucial spare parts for their submarines? My ranting distracted the officer from closely checking my papers, and he actually apologized for the inconvenience. I

asked him how I could acquire the special permit that was apparently missing without having to return all the way to my "home office" in Paris. He helpfully suggested that I should go to the *Oberkommando der Wehrmacht*, the high command of the army in Brussels, just half an hour from the border.

On the train back to Brussels, I chased two Belgian Hitler Youths out of the train compartment reserved for the German military and their civil servants. I felt compelled to do that. My strength was that I could use the Nazi bark quite convincingly.

It is impossible to describe how I felt. On the one hand, I knew full well who I really was, on the other, I had to slip into a totally different role. It was a matter of life or death. I was, of course, deeply conflicted about how to proceed, but decided eventually to go to the high command of the German Army in Brussels to apply for the missing special permit needed to cross the border back into the Netherlands.

The officer in charge told me to come back in an hour, because my request and my papers had to be checked. That was the most dramatic hour of my entire life! While walking through this beautiful park in Brussels, there were these two inner voices. One said: *You are crazy, this is bound to go wrong!*

The other voice replied: *What better choice do you have to offer?*

When I arrived back at the government building, the situation got even more dramatic. What did I see in front of it? One of the infamous green vans of the German riot squads! I thought it was waiting there for me . . ..

I went in and asked the officer, "Do you have my papers? Do you have my permit?"

The man behind the desk got up and said, "Just a moment." He disappeared into another room. Was he getting the Green Police? Agonizing minutes passed, during which I had to keep a straight face.

Finally, he returned with a friendly smile and said, "Everything is all right. Here are your documents. *Heil Hitler!*" I had an authentic special permit to cross the border, issued by the Wehrmacht! [1]

The original plan had been for Rudi to try to make his way from Spain to Portugal and on to England, where he wanted to enlist with the Dutch army-in-exile in order to join the Allied war effort and help liberate the continent. A little more than a week after he left, a neighbor called me to her phone (we were no longer allowed to have one). When I heard Rudi's voice, I wondered how he could call me from Spain. But he was at Amsterdam Central Station, greatly relieved that he had escaped with his life.

I was immensely grateful that he had returned unharmed and noticeably steeled by what he termed his "passage through hell." On the other hand, I had been looking forward to being just a sixteen-year-old schoolgirl for a while. Standing on tiptoe to keep up with my twenty-one-year-old boyfriend had been exhilarating, but also very demanding. I needed time to mature and did not feel ready yet to enter a lasting commitment. But thinking of our friends, relatives, and former neighbors in the camps, I realized how lucky I was, and we continued to make the best of our difficult situation.

After his return, Rudi reconnected with his contact in the Dutch underground. He learned he had been used as a guinea pig to test whether the counterfeit papers and stamps were airtight

Durchlaßschein West Nr. 74048
Laissez-Passer Ouest N° Holland

W. Deutsches Reich — Frankreich — Belgien

EDEL, Johannes Martinus
(Vorname, Familienname, Beruf)

aus   Amsterdam
(ständiger Wohnort, Straße, Hausnummer)

ist berechtigt, unter Vorlage des Passes — Passxxxxx — amtlichen
est autorisé, en présentant le passeport — la carte d'identité —
Lichtbildausweises — der Kennkarte ¹) —

Nr. 130897

ausgestellt von   Amsterdam   in der Zeit
délivré par

vom 13.Okt.   1943 bis zum 30.Okt.   1943
à partir du   jusqu'au

einmal¹) und zurück¹) —   X wiederholt¹)
une fois aller et retour

über die amtlich zugelassenen Übergangsstellen
à franchir les frontières par les passages officiels

von   Esschen
de

nach   Amsterdam/Holland
à

zu reisen

Brüssel , den 7.Okt.   1943
Der Generalquartiermeister
I. A.

¹) Nichtzutreffendes streichen.   Hauptmann

The authentic special permit for Johannes M. Edel to cross the Western border between Belgium and the Netherlands and could be used to send downed and rescued Allied pilots to southern France. The underground operatives wanted to know how well the connection with the French resistance had worked regarding helping fugitives to cross the Spanish border. About the *maquis* and the crossing of the Pyrenees, Rudi could not give a positive report. But the travel papers had proved to be excellent, and now they could be augmented by replications of Rudi's authentic border pass. That was a trump card in his hand. He negotiated with members of the Dutch resistance for additional counterfeit papers to secure his special-agent cover. Rudi did not attempt to leave the Netherlands again, but he never had to go back into complete hiding. He had suffered through that diminished existence for eleven months before his adventurous attempt to escape and was determined to try and survive in a less confined way.

On the strength of his documents, he was entitled to German military rations. Every other weekend, he boarded a train in the evening and traveled to a different small Dutch town. After office hours, he would register at the appropriate local command office to collect his special food ration coupons. Usually the only person around was a sleepy elderly soldier, who would casually study Rudi's papers and then hand him a food ration card and assign him a hotel for the night. Early the next morning, Rudi would return. At the first opportunity, he would pass the precious coupons on to me.

The German rations were much more generous than what was allotted to the Dutch population. It was embarrassing for me to walk into one of our neighborhood stores with food rationing coupons meant for the German enemy. Hence, I preferred to do the shopping a little farther from home. We put the butter, sugar, eggs, and other delicacies into packages and sent them to Rudi's parents in Westerbork.

Special travel paper issued to agents of the occupiers. The author and her father signed the diverse stamps.

The first six months after Rudi's return, he was employed in a woodworking factory in Diemen, not far from Amsterdam, to the southeast. He worked there with other men in hiding, most of them not Jewish. There were also a number of legal workers in the factory, which produced chairs and other wooden items for the German Army. Rudi slept on wood shavings in the crawl space under the factory, with machines running day and night. Luckily, he still had his bike that took him every other week to Amsterdam. He spent the weekend with my family, where he could take a bath and enjoy playing the piano. In the winter months, nightfall came early, and the streets would be dark because of blackout. Rudi could come and visit without fear of being recognized by former neighbors. There was a folding bed for him in our dining room, where he had also constructed a hiding place in a built-in closet, so he could disappear behind a cupboard in case of a surprise roundup. On Monday mornings, he had to leave again before daybreak.

Chapter Twelve

BAROGRAPH

✧ ✧ ✧

In the Netherlands, gifts are traditionally exchanged on the night of December 5, Saint Nicholas eve. In 1943, Rudi and I presented the family with a diary, the *Barograph*. Rudi had done the graphics, and in a long introductory poem, I explained the basic idea behind our "pressure recorder." From then until the end of the war, members of the household, including my grandmother Omi (who always had dinner with us), and Rudi, took turns writing a report about the week just past. We created an interesting record, and the cooperative effort shored up the flagging morale of the whole family. People often fell behind, but all the same, the *Barograph* bound us together.

Reporting on the week of January 16–22, 1944, my mother wrote that Rudi visited over the weekend, and everyone had enjoyed live chamber music. Mother and Rudi played four hands on her grand piano, and he accompanied her as she sang *Lieder* by Brahms, Schubert, and Hugo Wolf in her pleasing alto voice.

For the night of January 21, a year since we had been "Aryanized" and removed from the registration list, thanks to Hans Calmeyer, Mother made the entry, "We celebrated the first anniversary of the 'shedding of our stars' with a good bottle of wine."

The *Barograph* contains two graphs, one showing every-body's gradual weight loss between December 1943 and December 1944, as our food rations got smaller and smaller. The other graph traces everyone's mood swings.

There is a deep, deep low for Rudi on February 25, 1944, when his parents were deported from Westerbork. The blow was not unexpected. Practically all the Jews who had not gone into hiding had been rounded up by the previous fall. Most had been sent on to the East. Fewer and fewer patients came to the Westerbork infirmary, so the deferment stamp that had protected Rudi's father as an indispensable pharmacist was no longer valid.

A glimmer of hope remained, since we had learned there was a chance Rudi's parents would be sent to *Theresienstadt* (Terezin), a privileged destination as far as concentration camps were concerned. In their farewell letter, smuggled to Amsterdam on strips of toilet paper, Rudi's parents commended him to the love and care of my family. They took it for granted that I—age sixteen at the time—would be Rudi's companion through life. This assumption was both gratifying and daunting for me. Yet, I had no place or time to gain some distance. In the light of what was going on around me, my problems appeared minor. All we could dream of was survival. Everything else, we trusted, would fall in place once the war was over.

In the spring of 1944, Rudi no longer felt safe in the woodworking factory in Diemen. A regular worker had been boasting about his good and safe job in a factory that was not likely to be raided by the authorities since it produced goods for the German Wehrmacht. By then the days had grown longer, so Rudi's visits to my family for a much-needed shower, a good meal, some family comfort, and longed-for chamber music had to stop. Rudi quit his job and moved in with us temporarily until he found an address in Halfweg, halfway between the cities of Amsterdam and Haarlem, where a constable and his family took him in as a boarder under his false name. Rudi did not tell them he was Jewish, and they did not ask any questions.

By that time, it was clear that Germany was going to lose the war. Hopes were high that the defeat would come before the end of the year. Rudi began to prepare for the future by taking correspondence courses in radio technology. Luckily, he still had some money to tide him over. I biked or took the light rail to visit him at least twice a week. I remember wonderful walks among the large wheat fields in the *polder* (reclaimed land). My sisters and my mother also occasionally visited him that summer. Rudi had become part of the family.

Toward the end of the war, the "Calmeyer list" of temporary deferments shrank considerably. In March 1943, it bore 835 names; by November 1943, only 92.[1] Calmeyer took on an additional task, entailing new strategies and new kinds of lists. In German, the plurals of *Liste* (list) and of *List* (ruse) are identical: *Listen*. I cannot help but think that Calmeyer was aware of this tempting linguistic tidbit.

By 1944, half a million Dutchmen were performing unpaid forced labor in Germany. More men were needed. In cooperation with the Dutch Secretary-General of Internal Affairs, Mr. K. J. Frederiks (who would have to answer charges of collaboration after the war), Calmeyer suggested drawing up three new lists. There would be a black list of municipalities that had so far provided fewer than 10 percent of their eligible young men for labor in Germany; a silver list of municipalities that had provided more than 10 percent; and a gold list of municipalities that had provided the full 20 percent German authorities demanded. This was an elegant

and subtly-mocking way of stalling. Frederiks later remembered
the cooperation with Calmeyer as helpful and productive, which
indeed it was—particularly for the affected Dutchmen.

As the military situation grew more and more hopeless for
the Germans, the Nazis rightly claimed that their "Jewish Program" (Eichmann's term) in the Netherlands was a great success.
Of all the Jews who had lived in that country in 1940, 75 percent had been mass murdered, a singularly high percentage for
Western Europe. This "great success," as compared to that of the
elimination programs in Belgium and France, was partly due to
the fact that the occupied Netherlands had been under a civilian
rather than a military regime, the latter being more interested in
strategic matters than in controlling the population. The other
reason for the "success" was the superbly reliable Dutch bureaucracy, which the neighboring countries to the south could not
match.[2] Of the around twenty-seven thousand Jews who had
gone into hiding during the German occupation of the Netherlands, 60 percent survived.

Finally, on June 6, 1944, began the long-awaited Allied invasion in Normandy. The Western Allies made quick progress
through northern France and Belgium, and they crossed the
Dutch border in early September. We were afraid Amsterdam
would be laid under siege, so it seemed safer for Rudi to stay
with our family in Amsterdam rather than outside the city. He
arrived September 4, minutes before the ten p.m. general curfew.
The next day, *Dolle Dinsdag* (Crazy Tuesday) rumors reached
fever pitch: the Allies had broken through the German lines;
they would reach Amsterdam before nightfall. I joined hundreds
of people at the city's southernmost bridge, ready to greet our

liberators with a bouquet of flowers. Alas, our enthusiasm turned out to be premature.

Most unfortunately, the Allied forces were unable to hold their bridgehead on the northern bank of the River Rhine and lost control of the city of Arnhem. The country was cut in half: while the southern part of the Netherlands was liberated, the land north of the Waal River was still in German hands. On orders from the Dutch government-in-exile, the country's railroads went on a general strike on September 17, 1944, making it impossible for the occupiers to ship any more people and materials from the Netherlands to Germany. The German military responded by destroying the harbors of Rotterdam and Amsterdam and dismantling the Dutch railroad grid. The big cities in the west of the Netherlands were cut off from the coal mines in the southeast that provided the fuel for gas and electricity plants. Unless the Allies would liberate us soon, we faced a grim winter.

Chapter Thirteen

HUNGER WINTER

✤ ✤ ✤

The winter of 1944–1945 seared itself into Dutch memory as the *Hongerwinter*. Before the end of February 1945, at least eighteen thousand Dutch people died of starvation.[1] It was terrible to be both cold and hungry. Luckily, my father was able to provide us with a small one-burner stove, which Rudi set up in our living room, leading the stove pipe out through a ventilation flue. People tore the wood out of abandoned houses, many of them in the depopulated Jewish quarter. We bought some, and Rudi and I sawed it to size and chopped it up so it could be fed into the little stove on which we cooked for eight people: our family of five, my grandmother, and Rudi. The eighth person was an Austrian, Mrs. Scharwenka, who rented one of our attic rooms. Mother's grand piano doubled as our kitchen counter.

Most of all, I remember the darkness. Amsterdam is located on the 52nd parallel. In the depth of winter, we had no more than six hours of daylight. There were no batteries for flashlights, no candles. We had no paraffin or oil to burn. Rudi put one of our bicycles on a stand in the middle of our living room. He fixed two generators on the frame to light two bicycle lamps, one fastened to a music stand on the handlebar for the person pedaling, the other one clamped to the table, so that three people could huddle close and read. I was a senior in high school at the time and had a long list of books to read, so I usually volunteered to "ride the bike." The book I remember best reading while pedaling was the French biography of Madame Curie, written by her daughter Eve.

Our food rations dwindled. In December, I ventured out on a hunger trek with a neighborhood friend. Taking outgrown warm clothing and some table linens, we biked a little over fifty miles to Vierhouten and stayed at the Teunissens', bartering our textiles for wheat, butter, and eggs all along the way. That made for a nice Christmas dinner, especially welcome since Mother had fallen ill while I was gone.

The food situation grew worse, and our bicycle tires started to wear, with no replacements in sight. I joined people who dug fodder beets out of the fields. The heavy clay had to be washed off in the bathtub. They tasted nauseatingly sweet, yet they were more palatable than tulip bulbs, which I remember as bitter.

The successful German Christmas offensive in the Ardennes, known as the Battle of the Bulge, was a terrible setback, but the Russians were making steady progress toward the German border in the east. On New Year's Eve 1944, Rudi and I took a midnight walk through the frozen landscape feeling optimistic. From listening surreptitiously to BBC newscasts, we knew without a doubt that the new year would bring the end of the Third Reich.

All the while, school continued for at least a few hours every day in an unheated building. Our teachers tried to keep us interested, but attendance dropped drastically in the early months of 1945. Some parents sent their daughters to relatives in the countryside; other girls stayed home, miserable and sick. Our food rations were reduced to two hundred calories a day.

In February, Rudi combined our family's remaining bicycles into two useable conveyances, and my elder sister and I went on one more hunger trek to Vierhouten. Here are some excerpts of my report in the *Barograph*.

Sunday, March 3, 1945
"Vierhouten," a name that evokes two totally different images, for Vierhouten has long since been more than just a geographical location. There is the Vierhouten of 1941–42, where Rudi had taken refuge, the resting place and vacation place, where—surrounded by nature and peace—we laid the foundation of our friendship, even while in Amsterdam proscriptive decrees against the Jews followed each other in quick succession.

And now Vierhouten in the winter of 1944–45, one of the places of pilgrimage for starving city dwellers, Susi's and my destination last week when we biked there to obtain provisions for the whole family either by barter or by begging. . . .

[In one village] several well-to-do farmers and property owners pooled their resources and provided the city folks passing through with shelter for the night in a garage, with as much rye meal porridge as each could eat, and with a loaf of rye bread of almost 2 lb. to take along. . . . The van Ee family in Milligen [with whom Rudi had briefly hidden in the summer of 1941] put up from fifty to one hundred people in their barn every night . . . and the Teunissens, subsistence farmers or not, do not send away anybody asking for shelter, but rather offer everyone food in addition to a place to sleep. The Teunissens as well as the van Ees treated us as two out of the many who come and go, although they have known us for years; hence we obtained less food than we had hoped for.

So we had to sacrifice our own interests to the common good, which we gladly did even though circumstances have made us all selfish. . . . We often felt guilty when we got on our bikes after having repeated our litany of woe for the umpteenth time with varying success: "One loaf of bread and two pounds of potatoes a week and for both we have to stand in line for hours on end. No fuel, our father has TB and our mother was very ill earlier this winter, our little sister is in a growing spell and there is an old grandmother and Rudi, sitting cold and hungry near the stove, and we ourselves, who had always had enough food on the table, are now reduced to begging."

In the end, we no longer knew what was exaggerated. Then, leaving the highway of misery behind us, we would bike again through the forests we knew so well and yet could not enjoy the way we used to. . . .

One of the bikes—with a double set of poor tires—was very hard to pedal. All the provisions had to be loaded onto the other bike. On the way back, the westerly wind was so strong that [Susi and I] had to push our bikes part of the stretch.

When I review the last few weeks, I am absolutely sure that the worst is over! Everything points to a quick end. In the East, the Russians are moving towards Berlin. In the West, the Allies have reached Remagen [in Germany] and are poised to cross the Rhine; they are already occupying Cologne. Germany is under cruel bombing attacks. Unfortunately, the

Netherlands are also getting their share. The Hague has suffered badly from Allied bombardments. Thousands of people were killed. On the highways, too, more and more people are becoming victims of reckless shootings from strafing [Allied] airplanes.

Worst of all are the mass murders by the German SD (Security Police). Now that any chance of a German victory is gone, these monsters drag thousands of innocent people in the occupied territories along into the abyss, dubbing them "terrorists." In this respect, the last weeks have been the darkest ones of the war, yet in the larger scheme of things, this was probably bound to happen. The dreaded last straws . . . are heavy beyond words for those affected.

Here in the house, the *Barograph* curve rises with the mercury of the thermometer. . . .

Rudi is studying very diligently, and thanks to Mother's and Susi's incessant puttering, I also have more time to unwind and to do schoolwork. That feels good!

But what about our final matriculation examination? All we can do is wait and see. Let's not lose confidence! Worrying ahead of time is not helpful. We must be alert and make the best of it. That is all!

Hannes (my family nickname for Hansje / Hannelore).[2]

By February of 1945, malnutrition in the northwestern part of the Netherlands was so rampant that people were literally dying in the streets. The German occupiers feared an outbreak of contagious diseases such as typhus and cholera, which would threaten them personally. They allowed two Swedish ships to deliver thousands of tons of flour, margarine, and, if I remember correctly, also Portuguese sardines, to the port of Delfzijl in the northeast corner of the province Groningen, right at the German border. In my mind's eye I still see the large, amber-colored white bread Dutch bakers produced from the Swedish flour.

Four more shiploads followed. In early April, the northeastern part of the Netherlands was liberated. In Louis de Jong's *De Bezetting* (The Occupation), I read that Reich Commissar Seyss-Inquart had also authorized three trains daily to deliver potatoes to the Amsterdam, Rotterdam, and The Hague central community kitchens during the early months of 1945.[3] I only remember the potato peels in the thin soup one had to stand in line for, sometimes for hours.

In April 1945, Allied leaders, including U.S. Army Chief of Staff George Marshall, authorized Operation Manna (by the British Royal Air Force and the Royal Canadian Air Force) and Operation Chowhound (by the U.S. Army Air Forces). Speaking for a team of German officers including General Johannes Blaskowitz, the Wehrmacht Commander-in-Chief in the Netherlands, Dr. Seyss-Inquart agreed to a ceasefire within specified air corridors to allow a food drop. Between April 29 and May 8, the Allies dropped more than eleven thousand tons of food packages into the western part of the Netherlands. The packages lacked parachutes, so the pilots had to fly dangerously low, sometimes below balconies where Dutch civilians had gathered to wave at them. "Thanks Boys," the Dutch spelled out in tulip fields outside the cities. The German troops on the ground, mostly reduced to schoolboys and old men, honored their word: only two aircraft were lost due to a collision, and one due to an engine fire. A handful of bullet holes were found in some aircraft upon their return, apparently the work of individual soldiers.

My schoolmates and our teachers went up to the flat roof of our school to wave at the low-flying pilots. I remained behind in our classroom and cried my heart out. I just could not comprehend and accept that the same airplanes that dropped food for us during the day would at night drop incendiary bombs on seventeen-year-old girls in Germany, who were no more responsible for this horrible war than I was.

Chapter Fourteen

Liberation

✣ ✣ ✣

Finally, the war came to an end. According to a fabricated report, the Führer had died on the battlefield. The truth was that he ended his own life and that of his wife Eva Braun on April 30 in an elaborate underground bunker in Berlin. The devoted Joseph Goebbels did the same, killing also his wife Magda and their six children. Allied troops liberated the Netherlands on May 5, 1945.

Hitler had outlined a "scorched earth" policy to be implemented in the case of a German retreat. Had his orders been carried out, large parts of the Netherlands would have been flooded and The Hague destroyed. Seyss-Inquart, whom Hitler had designated in his "political testament" as the Reich's next secretary of state, disobeyed the orders. Returning from a brief meeting with Hitler's successor, Admiral Karl Dönitz, in Flensburg, Germany (which he could reach only by speedboat), Seyss-Inquart was arrested in The Hague on May 7.

It was my father's turn to report in the *Barograph* family diary about the week of May 1–8, 1945, the last days of the war. Under the date of May 1, he mentioned a capitulation offer by the German government (that is, by Heinrich Himmler), which Churchill was discussing in the House of Commons even as my father wrote. He continued: "In the meantime, the Allies keep moving forward; countless German cities have been conquered, including Munich and Regensburg; many German concentration camps that held hundreds of thousands of prisoners have been liberated. There are horrible reports about the conditions found in those camps, about mass murder and gruesome treatment of inmates."

On May 8, 1945, my father wrote: "Victory Day, the war in Europe is over, the Canadian troops moved into Amsterdam, the Germans are led away as prisoners of war." He described how the whole family went out to see the Canadian tanks roll into the city, then continued with what had happened four days earlier on Friday, May 4, when at nine p.m. all German units in the Northwest, including the Netherlands and Denmark, capitulated.

> We quickly organized a peace party including, besides the family, our closest neighbors and faithful friends. . . . I ceremoniously burned the yellow star with the word *Jood* [Jew] on it. The burning was meant as a symbolic act. May the world learn at long last that anti-Semitism originates with the enemy of mankind, who uses anti-Semitism to hide his dark, fiendish and reactionary machinations.[1]

When the German forces were at last defeated and a convoy of Canadian tanks drove through the jubilant city, Rudi and I were among the cheering crowd. We climbed onto a tank and celebrated with tens of thousands of others. I was seventeen, Rudi twenty-three. A few days later, a small delegation of our liberators visited my school. We had quickly learned the Canadian national anthem and rendered it with genuine abandon. I can still sing it now!

The first weeks after the delirium of liberation were very difficult. Friends and acquaintances who had survived in hiding surfaced pale, famished, and impoverished. Often a family member was missing—a child here, a wife there—who had been found, arrested, and deported by the Nazis. Those who emerged from hiding had only the worn clothing on their backs. Most of them were utterly dependent on support from others, often from relatives abroad.

In early June 1945, the first concentration camp survivors arrived by train in Amsterdam. Among them was Rudi's cousin, returning from *Theresienstadt* (Terezin). Ilse, a young woman of twenty-one and the only survivor of her family, was so traumatized that we soon learned not to ask her any questions about the camp and her parents.

Otto Frank also returned. Soviet troops had liberated him from Auschwitz and nursed him back to health. Mrs. Frank had died of exhaustion at Auschwitz, but the fate of their daughters was still unknown. Otto told us about the harrowing events he and his family had endured. Twenty-five months after they went into hiding, an unmarked car had appeared in front of Prinsengracht 263 on August 4, 1944. It is assumed that someone whose identity is still unknown called the German Security Police to report that illegal activities were going on in either the warehouse or the office spaces at the premises. Was it the man who had taken over for their reliable warehouse manager after the latter fell ill? Otto and the other people in hiding never trusted the replacement. Or was it a neighbor who caught a glimpse of movement through an attic window? Perhaps someone had noticed the many food deliveries to the office and hoped to collect the small bounty offered for betraying Jews in hiding.

The Franks and the others in the attic had been arrested, loaded into a van, and sent first to the Amsterdam jail, then to the transit camp Westerbork. One month later they were deported from Westerbork on the very last train bound for Auschwitz, a shipment of 1,091 Jews. Of these, 12 percent survived the camps, a relatively high percentage considering the fact that of the 108,000 Jews deported from the Netherlands to the concentration camps in 1941–1944, only roughly five thousand (less than 5 percent) returned.

Otto was happy to find our family intact, still in the apartment where he had last seen us three years earlier. We all hoped the Frank girls had survived at Bergen-Belsen, a camp that was by then known to have had no gas chambers.

We also anticipated that Rudi's mother was still alive. We had already learned that his father had been murdered at Auschwitz, but in August of 1944, two different Dutchmen, both forced into labor near Hamburg, Germany, had sent postcards to my family, telling us Rudi's mother had talked to them during air raids when their German guards took shelter. She wanted them to let us know she was part of a detachment of women ordered to clean up rubble after the heavy Allied bombardments. My mother immediately sent packages containing dried fruit, warm socks, a bar of soap, and whatever else we could spare, but we had no idea whether they ever reached Rudi's mother. As of mid-September 1944, following the general strike of the Dutch railroads, all mail connections to Germany had been cut off for us.

Because Rudi was so hopeful that his mother was still alive, he volunteered to join the International Red Cross immediately after we were liberated. The organization would not take him because he was stateless and without a passport, as were all German and Austrian Jewish refugees per Hitler's orders of November 1941. That made it hard to acquire a work permit and visa to travel abroad. The Red Cross had enough volunteers with valid passports to send as representatives to the liberated concentration camps. They made lists of the names of survivors. Rudi scanned these notices daily and eventually spotted his mother's name on a list of people the British had found alive in Bergen-Belsen.

Day after day Rudi and Otto Frank went to the Amsterdam Central train station to meet straggling survivors coming from the East. The two men held up photos of their missing loved ones. Finally, a woman returning from Bergen-Belsen told them that Margot and Anne had died of typhus at the camp in March or early April 1945, shortly before liberation. Otto Frank was heartbroken. He was the sole survivor of the eight who had hidden in the attic space above his business. Around the same time, Rudi learned that his mother had succumbed several weeks later, after Bergen-Belsen was liberated by British troops, who were much less adept at nursing starving inmates back to life than their Russian counterparts. Rudi was devastated since he had been so sure his mother would come back after seeing her name on a list of survivors. He had counted on building a new life for her and for himself, and now he was the sole survivor of his family, staring into a big void.

The same held true for Otto Frank. His trusted secretary, Miep Gies, had gathered up Anne's diaries and other manuscripts after the hiding place was raided. She handed them to Otto upon his return. He brought the folder full of papers to our apartment as he deliberated whether and what to publish. I remember him standing with Anne's manuscripts under his arm as my parents encouraged him to look for a publisher.

Chapter Fifteen

In Detention

✥ ✥ ✥

What is known as the "liberation" in the Netherlands is called the "capitulation" by the Germans. Anticipating their total defeat, most of the occupation officials had fled back to the Reich. To his credit, Hans Calmeyer elected to stay. He had never been a Nazi and did not fear retribution by the Allied or Dutch authorities. On behalf of his superior, Friedrich Wimmer, Calmeyer surrendered several departments of the Reich Commissariat to British and Canadian authorities.

On April 4, in his last letter home from the occupied Netherlands, he remarked to his mother in Osnabrück: "I have . . . no quarrel with my [recent] past. I even think I did not waste the last few years but did the right thing in the position I was assigned."[1] Several years later, Heinrich Miessen wrote to Calmeyer with satisfaction:

> "Our little office . . . was after all for many years under general suspicion all the way up to the National Security Main Office [in Berlin] and to the Party Headquarters. Hence it was routinely spied on,

according to frequent confidential warnings. Martin Bormann's Party Headquarters reproached us as early as 1943 for having unduly 'Aryanized' 16,000 Jews—at that time! In the summer of 1944 a blanket arrest warrant was issued, which fortunately could no longer be carried out since the advance of the Allies caused the SD to flee head over heels."[2]

The Dutch historian Louis de Jong estimated that by January 15, 1944, Calmeyer had increased the number of people crossed off the deportation lists from some 1,020 in March 1943 to 2,899. These were all people who had registered as Jews on the forms sent out in early 1941. In 1,868 other cases, Calmeyer had decided against the petitioner. Quite often these negative decisions concerned the Jewish partner in a "privileged mixed marriage," who was already exempt from deportation.[3]

Nonetheless, in the Netherlands, Calmeyer was seen and treated as a member of the defeated occupying forces. Immediately after the end of the war, the Dutch focused on identifying war criminals, collaborators, and "Jew catchers" among their own population. They set up new "political investigation offices," including special courts and people's tribunals, to handle the cases of sixty-nine thousand compatriots to be investigated and tried. Jails and prison camps were overcrowded. Internments were prolonged, and there was no such thing as a speedy trial.[4]

Calmeyer and other German officials remaining in the Netherlands were imprisoned under suspicion of having committed war crimes. They were first interned in Clingendael Manor in The Hague, the luxurious estate where Seyss-Inquart had resided. Three weeks later, they were moved to far more spartan facilities in Scheveningen, the *Oranje Hotel* as the Dutch called the forbidding prison near The Hague. It had most recently been used by the Germans for captured resistance workers, many of them patriotic supporters of the royal house of Orange. In the beginning, conditions were harsh. Internees were deprived of sleep and food, beaten, and robbed. Calmeyer estimated the value of objects stolen from him (including his wedding band) at 1,450 guilders, about US $362 in 1945, or a little over US $4,775 today. Most of all, he missed cigarettes.[5]

After about six weeks, conditions improved. Prisoners were allowed short walks, regular sports, and card games. Beginning in August 1945, they could see visitors. Calmeyer's longtime friend Wim Verkade as well as several Dutch lawyers who had represented Jewish clients during the occupation—including A. N. Kotting and Y. H. M. Nijgh (now Calmeyer's personal attorney)—paid visits. So did the Geel family, Calmeyer's landlords since he arrived in The Hague in 1941. They were the go-betweens for Calmeyer's correspondence with his family in Osnabrück while he was in custody.[6]

In his second book about Calmeyer, the German lawyer and politician Mathias Middelberg writes that soon after the German capitulation, when her husband was interned in the Netherlands, Ruth Calmeyer began to make rounds in Osnabrück seeking affidavits from recognized anti-Nazis who could vouch for Hans and were willing to do so in writing. Fortunately for Calmeyer, the couple had a well-defined set of friends who had opposed Hitler's regime from the outset, and Ruth was able to contact them.[7]

During his long detention, Calmeyer slept a great deal. He read magazines, English crime thrillers, and German novels. He ruminated on matters ranging from the history of law to the rules of right conduct. Calmeyer applauded Seyss-Inquart, Admiral Dönitz, and Albert Speer for disobeying Hitler's scorched-earth orders. The Reich Commissar had not inundated most of the western provinces of the Netherlands as the

Führer had ordered. "Once in a while a person bluntly says 'No!'. . . and prevails," Calmeyer wrote. "Overcome fear and you will have the upper hand."[8]

While Calmeyer's biographer Peter Niebaum attributed the long duration of Calmeyer's confinement to the enormous workload of the Dutch postwar political investigation offices, lawyer Ruth van Galen-Herrmann identified a more specific cause for the delay. In October 1945, a Dutch woman activist, the attorney Mrs. L. M. I. L. van Taalingen-Dols, filed a complaint against Calmeyer at the special court in The Hague. This lawyer held against Calmeyer that he had decided negatively on two cases she had brought before him during the war. On behalf of the court, the investigative lawyer Jeanne M. C. Romeijn set up pre-trial interrogations and an interview with Hans Calmeyer. Mrs. Romeijn eventually concluded there was no cause for trying Calmeyer in court.[9]

On April 11, 1946, Calmeyer was moved from cell 178 of the Scheveningen prison to the less onerous internment camp of Duindorp, in the same resort town. There he was interrogated several times. On April 16–17, 1946, he wrote the following statement:

> For a Dutch patriot, it may be hard to conceive that a German, although he stands in the strongest opposition to the regime of his country, will not easily decide to sabotage his government's measures during a time of war. It requires a moral law much more compelling than solidarity with his country to turn his criticism into actual sabotage. I want to emphasize that subsequently, a decent person should not pride himself on his acts of sabotage if he considered them necessary and morally justified. Therefore, do not demand from

me that for my justification I enumerate what, when, to what extent and how I sabotaged the anti-Jewish laws, what I undertook against the "occupying forces," and perhaps even why I did not go into hiding.

According to Ruth van Galen-Herrmann, the prosecutor, Mrs. Jeanne Romeijn, translated Calmeyer's pencil-written declaration from German into Dutch. A photocopy of this translation is in my possession. It is typed on official stationery of the Dutch Military Authority, Department of Criminal Investigation.

Strained though his relations with his wife often were, Hans Calmeyer no doubt appreciated her efforts to help secure his release from prison. In return, he sent encouraging thoughts, and he was eager to get home and to help build a new Germany. On May 9, 1946, Calmeyer wrote his last letter home from Duindorp:

Dear Ruth,

A few days ago, your letter of April 2 found its way directly to me. Till then I had to make do with greetings which the kindly Geels, Nijgh, [and other Dutch friends] passed on to me faithfully but infrequently. However, you should not lose your patience. Despite all understandable impatience, I always come back to the thought: "To be able to return home from this war in good health is more than one can ask for as a German." I have only one concern and that is to find the three of you alive and in good health when I come home. Everything else will fall into place.

I will return to you with so much zest for work, affirmation of life, and good health, as if I had not recently experienced a defeat but rather a personal victory. Hence, I rarely worry, and if I do, it is because I wonder how the three of you will see it through until my return. Your birthdays and Christmas must have been hard. That gives us the more reason to look forward to future special days once we are together again.

That is sure to happen, even though at this very moment it does not look as if the door will be opened for me within the next few days. They are easily distracted here. Since I do not like to be a spoilsport, my sense of humor usually helps me overcome the sluggish time, a belated and at this point rather outdated "time of military service."

Feel embraced with much love, wait patiently, remain healthy and brave, partake of any kind of good cheer this period has to offer, because that is the only way to overcome it. . . .

It would not be a bad idea for a reasonable Briton to request your Hans for Hanover [headquarters of the British occupying forces in Northwest Germany after the war].

One must push a little when initiative is lacking. Thanking you, embracing you, and kissing you; stay well,

Your Hans[10]

On July 28, 1946, after more than a year in detention, he found comfort in the following reflections:

I have learned that my mother, my wife and son are healthy. I myself made it through the last thirteen years with my limbs intact and my spine unbroken. During this accursed war, good fortune enabled me to save the lives of a number of people, and I did not have to shoot anybody. I caused nobody's misery; nobody's blood is staining my fingers. Don't I have reason to be glad!?![11]

In July 1946, Mr. J. Zaaijer, the Dutch Attorney General and prosecutor at the Special Court, declared that any suspicion Calmeyer had committed war crimes was unsubstantiated. Most likely, the case was reviewed over the summer.[12]

On September 4, 1946, Dr. Paul Merdinger wrote a statement in support of Hans Calmeyer. Merdinger identified himself as an Austrian, an anti-Nazi as of 1934, and a former concentration camp inmate. He recounted how he had met Hans Calmeyer in The Hague in 1942, at a time when the German lawyer held a crucial position in the Reich Commissariat. He knew Calmeyer, he said, not only as a keen anti-Nazi, but as a truly good German. By now, he added, very few of these were left.

Merdinger testified that he could not begin to enumerate the many things Hans Calmeyer had done for the Dutch population and hence for the Dutch state, and indirectly also for the Allied cause. Together with his Dutch friends, he thanked Mr. Calmeyer for saving at least ten thousand human lives.

Merdinger and his friends were ashamed, he wrote, that the investigation into Calmeyer's case was taking so long. In closing, he expressed gratitude and admiration for Hans Calmeyer's rare political genius. As an idealist, a true socialist, and a German patriot of long standing who did his utmost during the Nazi period, Calmeyer deserved the very best for his future endeavors in Germany. The testimony was signed: Dr. Paul Merdinger, editorial correspondent of *Je Maintiendrai* ("I Will Maintain," an underground Dutch resistance newspaper during the occupation years and the motto of the Netherlands).[13]

Merdinger's testimony was written in English, though somewhat awkwardly (hence the indirect quotation above), presumably so it might help Hans Calmeyer secure a useful position at the offices of the British occupying forces in Hanover. In his May 9 letter home (quoted above), Calmeyer had expressed interest in such a position. Striking in this letter, as well as in his subsequent reflections of July 28, are his positive view of himself and his eagerness to spring into action.

Chapter Sixteen

NEW BEGINNING

✣ ✣ ✣

At last, in mid-September 1946, Hans Calmeyer was freed and could return to his family. He was forty-two when the war ended and forty-three before he returned to Germany. Coming by train via Münster, Calmeyer arrived in Osnabrück at midday on September 15, 1946. It must have been traumatic to find a city of bomb-wrecked buildings and people whose lives were in shambles. The country had been physically and morally destroyed. People preferred not to ask any questions. What they wanted was enough food and shelter, economic and political stability, security, and restoration.

Following up on his intentions to serve his country under the aegis of the British Commonwealth Occupying Force, one of the first things Calmeyer did upon his return to Germany was to write a short but revealing autobiography for the purpose of introducing himself. Under the English heading, "What About Calmeyer?" he wrote in German, using the present tense and referring to himself in the third person. After a short sketch of his upbringing and studies and his early anti-Nazi stance, he continued:

The first day of war finds him a soldier. As a member of an air communication company he first serves at home then, starting in May 1940, in the Netherlands. In March 1941, the jurist is called from the troops to serve in The Hague at the Office of the Reich Commissar as a temporary scientific assistant to the Commissioner General for Internal Affairs and Justice. C. succeeds in ameliorating orders and demands, in mitigating them, or in implementing them in such a way that freedom, property, and life of the people in the occupied country are respected. By pure chance C. is tasked to decide doubtful cases ensuing from the decree by the Reich Commissar regarding the compulsory registration of Jews and half-breeds. Thus he (a fundamental and bitter opponent of the German laws against the Jews) is assigned the quasi-judicial classification of borderline cases. For malicious tongues in the Office of the Reich Commissar, C. becomes the "Jews' Calmeyer"; the Commissioner General for the SS and for Security in the Netherlands, Himmler's representative there, calls him "protector of all Jews" and "saboteur of the laws against the Jews." Perhaps it is the unspoken respect of the many spineless colleagues for the outsider and non party member that makes it possible for C. to keep his assignment, which, in turn, allows his decisions to stand.

In the Netherlands the net result of his endeavors is easily assessible. He may have been able to save around 17,000 human lives. Not enough, if he were to be asked. In Germany his value may be the unbroken spine he managed to preserve for himself through twelve years of National Socialism.

The Germans who apostatized from Europe, who idolized violence, can only be led back to the Western community by people who, rather than believing in machine guns, put their faith in the law. This "law" is not only a limit set against arbitrariness for utilitarian reasons. It is a humanitarian ideal, an inalienable claim, and a moral possession of the individual who demands the application of "law" for himself and others.

The demoralization caused by twelve years of the Hitler regime... has prepared the [typical] German to exchange one idol for the next Baal. Only those Germans who were immune against the first poison can safeguard their compatriots against a second epidemic.[1]

Hans Calmeyer in the late 1940s

We know of no immediate response on the part of the British authorities. Calmeyer went about adjusting to life in devastated postwar Osnabrück as best he could. He set up a law office in two rooms of the duplex his parents had built at Friedrichstrasse 48. His mother continued to live there with Hans, Ruth, and their son Peter. A refugee woman had also been quartered with the family.

In addition to practicing law, Calmeyer acquired a license to work as a notary. Office duties frequently took him to the homes of farmers in the area around the city. His immense patience in explaining legal issues was often rewarded with payments in kind. He and his neighbor and friend Max Berling planted tobacco in the garden of their shared house to help counter the shortage of cigarettes.

The winter of 1946–1947 was extraordinarily harsh, with average temperatures of –15 degrees Celsius (5 degrees Fahrenheit) and low temperatures of –28 degrees Celsius (–18 degrees Fahrenheit). On December 15, Calmeyer wrote to his prewar Osnabrück friend Karl Fritz Erdmann, who now lived in the Black Forest area after three months of incarceration by the Germans in occupied France for "subversion and defeatism":

> The desolate sight of nothing but ruins (which applies not only to churches and houses but equally to human beings) is discouraging even for a person who has returned from the adventure of the last seven years infused with vigor and good intentions. And the sight does not recede; day after day it attaches itself to a person.[2]

Calmeyer was conscious of his privileged position. In a later letter to Erdmann, written March 7, 1947, he said, "My family and I are so much better off than many compatriots that it behooves me to be grateful and cheerful." All the same, he found his home city "desolate and discouraging."[3]

Sixty million people had died in the war, almost half of them Soviet Russians. Six million of the dead were European Jews who had been systematically murdered. Hundreds of thousands of people were missing and unaccounted for—tracing services would be active for decades. The war had left behind two million injured and half a million orphaned, along with more millions of displaced persons (DPs), camp survivors as well as those who had been forced into slave labor for Hitler's Germany, then released with no food or shelter.[4]

The statistics in Germany were bleak. Three million apartments had been destroyed, or 41 percent of the country's living quarters. One-third of Germany's rail lines and one-half of its engines and freight cars had to be scrapped. Four hundred million cubic meters of rubble awaited removal.

Crime was rampant and famine severe. People who still owned something worth exchanging took it to the countryside to barter with farmers for basic foods. Public utility networks in the cities had been destroyed or disrupted. The German people stole coal from freight trains and used peat or coal dust from nearby mines for heating.[5]

By the fall of 1945, a ban on political activities within the British occupation zone had been lifted, as well as a ban on direct interaction between Britons and Germans. In Osnabrück, the British occupation authorities appointed a citizens' committee to serve as a provisional city council. It consisted only of non-Nazis, among them people Hans Calmeyer knew well, such as Friedel Rabe, an acquaintance from the USPD (the United German Socialist Party), and Bruno Hanckel, the leftist bookstore owner from his prewar circle of friends. In October, the British authorities appointed colleague Wilhelm Rosebrock, Calmeyer's close friend and roommate from the internship days of their legal training (the one who wished to be hanged from the same tree as Calmeyer), to act as mayor of the city.

Osnabrück's previous enthusiasm for Hitler and for National Socialist policies lay near the surface, though. When Bruno Hanckel dared to decorate the windows of his bookstore with newspaper clippings featuring photographs of now-denounced former Nazi notables, indignant fellow citizens smashed the window glass.

Yet orchestras and theaters started up again, performing in the ruins of the former theater building and in a covered flower hall. Thornton Wilder's *By the Skin of Our Teeth* was on one of the first playbills. With two-thirds of the old inner city destroyed, the people who had survived by the skin of their teeth filled the churches to capacity during Sunday morning services. Authorities proclaimed a citywide cleanup action to start clearing away rubble, to repair dwellings, and to rebuild the inner city. Everyone was ordered to help.[6]

Chapter Seventeen

DENAZIFICATION

✤ ✤ ✤

While he was still in Dutch custody, Calmeyer had learned that his old antagonist, Commissioner General Hanns Albin Rauter, had been charged, convicted, and executed in the liberated Netherlands. In that country, thirty-eight death sentences had been carried out.

But how was Germany to reverse course? The Allied powers occupying the vanquished country instituted a program of "denazification" aimed at excluding those with a Nazi past from positions of power and influence in postwar society. Former party members and others suspected of supporting or assisting the Nazis were required to fill out questionnaires about their activities during the Hitler years.

Hans Calmeyer followed the trials and the endless discussions of their every aspect in the press and on the radio. In 1946, suspects were slotted into five categories:

(1) *major offenders*, subject to immediate arrest followed by imprisonment or death;

(2) *offenders* (including activists and profiteers), subject to immediate arrest and imprisonment with labor for up to ten years;

(3) *lesser offenders*, subject to probation without internment for two to three years;

(4) *followers* (fellow-travelers), subject to fines and possible restrictions on employment, travel, and political rights; and

(5) *persons exonerated*, subject to no sanctions.

Further restrictions applied to those in the first three categories—for example, they could not publish newspapers or magazines, teach in schools or universities, hold important positions in business or industry, or serve as public officials.

At the Nuremberg Trials, Dr. Arthur Seyss-Inquart was tried along with twenty-three other major war criminals during the first of thirteen International Military Tribunal (IMT) sessions held between 1945 and 1949. The panel consisted of eight judges, two from each of the four victorious Allied powers: the United States, Great Britain, France, and the Soviet Union. The first trial lasted ten months. Hitler and two of his highest-ranking associates, Joseph Goebbels and Heinrich Himmler, had committed suicide (the former two in Hitler's Berlin bunker) just before Germany's capitulation.

The Allies used new technology to provide simultaneous translations in German, French, English, and Russian through headphones. After hundreds of testimonies in four different languages, all but three of the accused were found guilty. Twelve were sentenced to death (one, Hitler's powerful private secretary Martin Bormann, was missing and sentenced in absentia). The others were punished with prison terms ranging from ten years to life. Hermann Goering, head of the Luftwaffe, was sentenced to death. He committed suicide the night before the executions. Ten of the condemned were hanged in October 1946 in less than two hours. Arthur Seyss-Inquart was the last of them.

Albert Speer, Hitler's thoughtful, much admired architect and minister of armaments, was sentenced to twenty years in prison. Though many supporters called for his early release, he served the full term at Spandau Prison in Berlin. Speer was the only defendant at Nuremberg who took personal responsibility for his actions. In the course of his trial, he delivered a warning:

"A new great war will end in the annihilation of human culture and civilization. Once technology and science are unleashed, there is nothing to prevent the destruction of mankind. Therefore, this trial must be a contribution toward the prevention of future depraved wars and the establishment of ground rules for human coexistence."

Grand Admiral Karl Dönitz, Hitler's designated successor, was sentenced to ten years at Spandau Prison. In his defense, he declared he had trusted the Führer principle—that the Führer alone, the leader of the people, defined the law. Yet, he admitted that when this principle entailed such appalling consequences, something must be wrong with it.[1]

The first trial of the major war criminals from November 20, 1945, to October 1, 1946, was followed by a second series of twelve trials by the International Military Tribunal between 1946 and 1949, again in Nuremberg. . . . Sixteen "racial purity" jurists were charged in one trial, and in another, "racial cleansing" and "resettlement" officials. Others arraigned were physicians, generals, corporate directors, and *Einsatzkommandos* (special task forces). Not all were found guilty; twelve further culprits were condemned to death, eight to life in prison, and seventy-seven to prison terms of various lengths.[2]

Like the theologian Martin Niemöller and the philosopher Karl Jaspers, Calmeyer held the opinion that the Germans were not collectively guilty, but rather collectively *responsible* for what took place during the Nazi years. Twenty years later, writer and political theorist Hannah Arendt would deem it the "essence of moral confusion" that "in postwar Germany those who were completely guiltless would assure each other and the whole world how guilty they felt, whereas only few of the actual criminals were ready to show even the smallest trace of contrition."[3]

As the Allied authorities handed over more and more responsibility for running the country to the Germans, the task of "denazifying" Germany devolved to the country's own authorities. The Allies issued no guidelines as to procedures and criteria for denazification. Execution of the program varied from region to region according to the political purposes of the occupying nation. The Americans considered every German over the age of eighteen complicit with the Nazis and sought to reeducate for democracy, while the Soviets aimed to nationalize property and to promote communism. The French wanted to weaken Germany, their traditional enemy. The British stressed the need for economic development in Germany and were generally inclined to leniency.[4]

The number of cases to be resolved was impossibly large. By early 1947, the Allies held ninety thousand Germans in detention. Another two million were prohibited from working at anything other than manual labor. Meanwhile, Germany desperately needed experts—trained teachers, technical workers, lawyers and judges, and workers skilled in every trade. Restrictions were gradually relaxed, and commitment to denazification eroded.[5]

Local authorities set up hundreds of special tribunals, making the judicial process faster and more efficient, but less rigorous. The tribunals began accepting statements from witnesses regarding the pre-1945 involvement of the accused in National Socialist activities. Popularly called *Persilscheine* ("white-washing certificates," after the whitening laundry detergent *Persil*), these statements helped prepare the way for reclassifications, amnesties, so-called rehabilitations, and reinstatements to public and private positions initially barred to anyone with a Nazi past.[6]

After Germany's 1945 capitulation to the Allies, there had been much talk of a "zero hour"—a decisive new beginning cleansed of the Nazi stain and devoted to democratic values of truth and freedom. However, in the new republic, based on majority rule, ideas from the Hitler era soon resurfaced. In West Germany at war's end, that majority consisted of erstwhile Nazi supporters or fellow travelers, plus the politically indifferent. Operative social structures had scarcely changed. By 1948, attention had turned to the Cold War and to growing tensions between the Eastern bloc and its Western counterpart. To the frustration of erstwhile anti-Nazis, Calmeyer included, the shame of the Nazi years was swept under the carpet.

Novelist Günter Grass spoke of his disappointment as postwar Germany resettled into old patterns:

> There was a hope, an extravagant hope [for a new beginning]. But since everything that was started culturally was shortly again hemmed in by old and new political and economic considerations, there was, of course, no zero hour. The same economic forces that brought Hitler to power in 1933 and before 1933 were there again, with almost unbroken vitality. The NSDAP (Nazi Party) had . . . more than six million party

members. Those were not gone, but denazified.... The few people who had offered resistance, those who had emigrated then returned from abroad, would—it was believed—be able to set up a "different Germany" [the cliché integral to the concept of the zero hour]. These hopes were deceptive. The structures that seemed to be terminated by the unconditional capitulation reappeared within a short time.[7]

Like many Jews, acclaimed writer Alfred Döblin had fled to France in 1933 and from there on to the United States. He returned to Germany almost immediately after the war, only to emigrate back to France in 1953. The once politically *engagé* writer was disappointed that the Germans seemed to have learned nothing. In 1946, Döblin expressed his dismay about the state of affairs in Germany:

Here lives, unchanged, a hardworking people of orderly habits. As always, they have been obedient to a government, latterly to Hitler, and in general, they do not understand why, this time, being obedient should have been wrong. It will be much easier to rebuild their cities than to get them to understand what they have undergone and how it came to pass.[8]

Döblin echoed the opinion of American journalist William L. Shirer, who attended the first of the Nuremberg Trials and observed in Berlin in 1945: "They [the Germans on trial] do not have any guilt feelings and regret only that they have been beaten and that they now have to take the consequences. They are sorry only for themselves, not for all the people they have murdered and tortured.[9]

Prominent thinkers discussed guilt and responsibility. Pastor Martin Niemöller published the "Stuttgart Confession of Guilt by the Protestant Church" in October 1945, and in the same year philosopher Karl Jaspers discussed guilt in his lectures and in a brochure "The Question of Guilt." To Calmeyer's dismay, the questions of guilt and responsibility, which should have concerned all Germans, did not interest the great majority. Some former accomplices clung to Nazi ideology; others were fully engaged in the struggle for survival and had no time for introspection. Eager to return to prewar prosperity, most Germans did not ponder the possibility of a new moral life.[10]

Both politically and economically, the old elites remained in power. Investigators had recommended the liquidation of the big banks and industrial corporations that had cooperated with Hitler to their own profit. But even these entrenched institutions survived and continued to thrive.

Chapter Eighteen

WHERE TO FIT IN?

✤ ✤ ✤

At the end of 1946, Calmeyer was asked by the Osnabrück inspector for the Office of Denazification, a Mr. Goers, to preside over a denazification tribunal. Calmeyer declined the position in a letter dated January 13, 1947:

> The damage already done can only be ameliorated by a far-reaching amnesty. There is an urgent need for amnesty. If, however, it is granted because of the embarrassing failure of the present determination of guilt, then amnesty loses all its healing effect. Amnesty must be an act of confidence. A person who places confidence, acquires confidence. . . . The denazification process in its present form leads to degradation wherever even minor incriminatory evidence is found. That would not be so bad if it applied only to a small circle of persons who are really guilty. However, we are dealing with a very large circle—"one cannot degrade two-thirds of the German people"—and the result is particularly devastating since the whole population of

Germany has already been degraded, both economically and socially, by [years of] armament, war, and
bombardments. Degraded once again, a person will
be more discouraged, more desperate, and, alas, even
more self-righteous and unreasonable than a person
who carries his burden of guilt—be it acknowledged
or not—together with his share of Germany's economic bankruptcy.

Let me assure you that I do not like to decline
the call to serve; yet I believe that I cannot be useful
in the position I have been offered but might rather
prove harmful.

Hans Calmeyer
Lawyer[1]

Despite the businesslike tone of Calmeyer's letter to the
inspector, his disappointment in the denazification process is
palpable.

Another source of disillusionment soon after his return
from the Netherlands, was Calmeyer's relationship with his wife.
In the spring of 1947, Ruth traveled to Switzerland to seek a
cure for kidney problems. She had a lover there. When Calmeyer
received an offer from Hanover, the capital of Niedersachsen (the
state of Lower Saxony that includes Osnabrück), to take a leading
position in the Department of Cultural Affairs, he was eager to
accept. In a letter of October 7, 1947, Hans implored Ruth to
return from Switzerland and accompany him to Hanover.[2] She
declined, leaving it to her husband to decide whether he wanted
the assignment badly enough to go alone.

More likely than not, these two basic disappointments set
the tone for Hans Calmeyer's life after the war. All too soon,

little was left of the eagerness for a constructive role in rebuilding his country and of the zest for life expressed in his last letter home from Dutch internment.

Calmeyer had access to the world of art, particularly to that of literature, which was to become his refuge when he found himself unable to make a meaningful contribution to his country's rise from its ashes. Already in his letter of December 15, 1946, to his friend Erdmann, Calmeyer referred to his own incarceration in terms of Thomas Mann's cycle of novels *Joseph and His Brothers*, ending his reflection with a quotation from the poet Rilke.

> In any case, I for one . . . am convinced that no one is thrown into a pit for any reason other than to arise from it again to a new, different, and even better life. . . . It does not really matter for which "coat of many colors" we are thrown in by our brothers. More important is what we derive from it spiritually. First in the pit, and then afterward. . . . [T]hat which is uncompromised has remained much more marvelously intact and deserves to be praised. "To praise, that is it."[3]

Thomas Mann had long been one of Calmeyer's favorite authors. As a student in Jena, he had jotted down a quotation from *The Magic Mountain*: "Passion is to live for the sake of life. . . Passion, that is, forgetting oneself."[4]

Despite marital tensions, Calmeyer believed that wedding vows were for life, and he did not intend to dissolve his marriage. He wrote long letters to his wife during the months she was in Switzerland seeking help for her health problems. In a letter of August 27, 1947, he reported glowingly about their son Peter, now seventeen, who was developing into a thoughtful and observant young man. He himself was managing, he said, helped by his sense of humor and by the memory of the "lifeboat" he was once able to cobble together, though his vision of himself as "an angel of the Lord" had proved to be an illusion.[5]

In his long letter of October 7, in which he told Ruth about the position he had been offered in the Department of Cultural Affairs in Hanover, he also wrote of other matters: a concert he had attended, and the visit of his "nieces" Renata and Ilse (in reality they were more distantly related), who had spent a brief vacation at the house in Osnabrück. In addition, he mentioned Ruth's niece Ines Hentschel, who was "taking loving care of him."[6]

Ines, the same age as the Calmeyers' son, had been Peter's playmate as a child. She was the daughter of Ruth's sister, Ilse Tribius Hentschel. Ines was employed in Calmeyer's law office as a *Lehrling* (apprentice) in the German tradition of learning an occupation through two or three years as an intern on the job. She also helped out in the household.

After Ruth declined her husband's urgent plea to go with him to Hanover, Calmeyer decided to proceed alone. Though not looking for a career change, he was eager to try his hand on a temporary basis at helping to shape postwar Germany's cultural policies. In Hanover he worked under Adolf Grimme, the secretary of cultural affairs, who had been a member of the "Red Orchestra," an active German resistance organization during the Nazi era. Grimme was known to handpick his staff according to each individual's conduct under the Nazi regime, so Calmeyer found himself working among like-minded people.

Meanwhile, Britain, France, and the United States were finding it increasingly difficult to cooperate with Stalin and the Soviets in occupied postwar Germany. After a series of conferences in London between February and June 1948, the Western

Allies decided to combine their three zones of occupation into a separate West German nation in order to administer the new state as a single economic unit and to reform the German currency. The adoption of the *Deutsche Mark* (DM) at the birth of the Federal Republic of Germany (FRG, popularly known as West Germany), amid rising tensions with Stalin, provoked the devastating blockade of West Berlin between mid-June 1948 and May 1949. This blockade was the first major international incident of the Cold War.

Calmeyer left Hanover in the fall of 1948, shortly after the currency reform. His resignation was—at least in part—prompted by the fact that his law office was suffering from his absence. Moreover, there was a reshuffling of the government in Hanover, which may have caused some disenchantment. Grimme thanked him with warm words of appreciation: "For almost a full year, you have been the head of the Art Department, a position that requires particularly reliable cultural refinement, human and artistic insight, flexibility, and at the same time self-assurance." Grimme emphasized that it had been extremely difficult to find the right person to fill that delicate yet crucially important position, and Calmeyer had done a superb job.[7]

After both Hans and Ruth returned to Osnabrück, Ruth actively helped to organize his law office on Friedrichstrasse. Their business partnership was practical and suited them both. Ruth managed employees, money, and time better than Hans did, and she assisted him with the day-to-day running of his affairs. His reflective, reclusive side (perhaps also the company of other women in the office) allowed him to distance himself when he found his wife overbearing.

In the late 1940s, Calmeyer issued several *Persilscheine*, the laundering certificates for people facing the denazification process. He was happy to provide an exonerating character reference for his former staff member in The Hague, Heinrich Miessen, who had helped him save many Jewish lives despite being a party member. But there were other cases like that of Willy Münzer, who had been the prewar head of the Nazi Party for the Osnabrück district and, during the war, commissioner for the province of Zeeland in the occupied Netherlands. Münzer headed for Calmeyer's office on Friedrichstrasse for legal advice, when he was facing a denazification probe. He had known about Calmeyer's rescue operation in The Hague and could have exposed him to the SD/SS but refrained. All the same, when Ruth caught sight of him, she vociferously threw him out, telling him never again to set foot in the house. Münzer made a second attempt to meet with Calmeyer, this time managing to bypass the lawyer's wife. Calmeyer advised him to tell the truth during the probe.[8]

In subsequent years, Calmeyer prepared numerous requests for reparations and compensations due to victims of Nazi injustice. He also worked on many divorce cases, earning the reputation of being a reconciliation lawyer rather than a divorce lawyer. His sympathies were with the children from broken marriages.[9]

A second Ruth, Ruth Mnich, also worked in Calmeyer's law office in the early postwar years. Born in Silesia, she was a refugee from the Oder-Neisse area (the Oder and the Neisse rivers had become the border between Germany and Poland after 1945). Mnich deemed her boss amiable, very friendly, yet given to the impulse to lecture. On the other hand, she observed, he was totally ignorant of the world. "A child!" she said. He had to be constantly reminded not to leave his coat or official robe hanging somewhere, or to take along a handkerchief or some pocket change for a cup of coffee on court days.

When it came to the annual office outing, the office troupe had to go to the Netherlands; there simply was no other destination for Calmeyer. Despite this minor quirk, his office employees saw him as a fairy-tale boss who did not lose his temper but patiently explained, often praised, recommended books and films, and encouraged continued education.[10]

His staff frequently felt embarrassed by Ruth's incessant needling of her husband, which could become unbearable when she was under the influence of alcohol. Calmeyer himself never drank. His coworkers had the distinct impression that he could not get angry, even if he tried.

As a compensation for legal work, Calmeyer had received a longhaired dachshund he named Joker. The dog preferred his company to his wife's. Since Ruth suffered from kidney troubles, she liked to sit in her office chair with Joker, a living hot-water bottle, against her back. The dog, however, was eager to run over to Hans, who treated him tenderly and took him for long country walks.[11]

A young lawyer named Rolf Gurland joined the law office in 1952. He reported that he and Calmeyer shared the belief that the struggle for justice was always worthwhile, even if the material value at stake was minuscule. Gurland later became Calmeyer's business partner.[12]

Chapter Nineteen

UNCHARTED FUTURE

✤ ✤ ✤

In the summer of 1945, while Calmeyer was in custody in Scheveningen waiting to start his postwar existence, Rudi Nussbaum attempted to put his life together. Now that he knew that his mother would not return, he was on his own, a young man of twenty-three without even a high school diploma.

Once the international postal services resumed, he received warm and supportive mail from his mother's younger sister in Johannesburg, South Africa. Aunt Marie and her husband were childless. They wanted Rudi to study chemical engineering, hoping that upon completion of his training he would move to South Africa and enter his uncle's paint factory as a technical expert.

Rudi had applied at several Dutch radio stations for an internship as a sound engineer, but no one wanted to hire stateless persons. Their status was unclear, since *Militair Gezag*, the temporary military Dutch government, had declared stateless people Germans again. Some of them remained locked up in Westerbork, together with Dutch Nazis. Refugee survivors returning from *Theresienstadt* (Terezin) were temporarily interned near Maastricht with the intent to ship them across the border of their erstwhile home country as soon as feasible. There was an outcry of protest, and by mid-July stateless people who had been issued a resident's permit before the war were allowed to resettle in the Netherlands. Since Rudi's relatives were willing to send him a small monthly stipend as he pursued his education, he decided to get his high school diploma and then enter the Technical Institute of Higher Learning in Delft.

Throughout the Netherlands, students of the class of 1945, to which I belonged, were given high school diplomas without sitting for the matriculation examination. During the school year 1944–1945, seventeen- or eighteen-year-old boys in the still-occupied parts of the country had been well advised not to go to school for fear that the occupation authorities would swoop down and take them to Germany for forced labor. Most girls in my senior class had quit school. Some had been sent to live with relatives in the countryside, where there was still some food; others were too malnourished or too dispirited to make the effort. In the end, as in my Jewish school a little over two years earlier, only five or six students were left in my class.

When the announcement came that we would receive our diplomas without having to pass the national examination, my classmates were jubilant. I smiled but could not really share their relief. Being a schoolgirl and studying, even cramming for exams, had been an attractive prospect for me, since it would afford a legitimate excuse to avoid facing the overwhelming sadness of those first postwar months. In addition to our Jewish relatives and friends who had not survived the war, many helpers, including Mrs. Blokland (in whose house Rudi had stayed for almost a year) and Mr. Rijkers (the owner of the wood factory who had employed Rudi and many other illegals), had been found out and had paid with their lives for saving those of others.

Once school was dismissed, I had no trouble finding a job as a junior reporter for the department of social affairs of *Het Vrije Volk* (The Free People), a social democratic daily that had newly emerged from the underground. I had always enjoyed writing. Since my parents had barely scraped by during the last years of the war and my father was still casting about to start a new business, it seemed only fair to me that I should contribute to our living expenses. Meanwhile, Susi and I tutored Rudi in Dutch literature and Dutch history to make sure that the coming September he would be admitted to register as a high school senior.

Rudi was by far the oldest student in his high school class. But there were others who had gone through unusual experiences during the war, and soon Rudi got to enjoy this year as a schoolboy and did very well. He often walked to school with my younger sister. Although eight years his junior, Marli was just two years behind Rudi in school. The stipend from his uncle and aunt allowed Rudi a season's subscription to the *Concertgebouw* Orchestra. More than anything else, music helped him to find his bearings.

Meanwhile, as a fledgling journalist, I was clipping news stories from other newspapers, reporting on meetings called by a variety of organizations as regular life started up again, and writing my own little pieces. One contribution went with a picture of a recently discovered makeshift burial mound with a German and an Allied helmet attached to the marker. I waxed quite poetic about the pernicious concept of "enemy" as the guiding principle for soldiers who are taught to hate, fear, and kill their unknown counterparts.

After three months, however, I grew disenchanted with my job at the newspaper. I had been sent to the Amsterdam harbor to report on a stevedores' strike. After interviewing a Social Democratic dockworker, whose union was against the strike, and his Communist colleague, who was strongly in favor of it, I wrote a carefully balanced report. The next day, my paper published only the opinions of the Social Democratic stevedore. That did not sit well with me, since I did not want to toe the party line. With the aplomb of an eighteen-year-old, I decided I had better go to college and gain knowledge and prestige so that, in the future, people would have to publish what I wrote.

Just when I was about to quit my job, I learned of a Quaker boarding school near Ommen, in the eastern part of the Netherlands. It had been founded before World War II to give the children of diplomats stationed in Germany an education not predicated on the Nazi world view. Many Jewish children had been sent there while their parents were trying to obtain visas to go overseas. The classes were conducted in English, and students sat for the Oxford School Certificate as their final exam. The school had been closed toward the end of the war but was now reopening with a handful of students. It seemed an ideal place for me to catch my breath and read to my heart's content. Besides, the school offered Latin, which I had not had the opportunity to study before.

The costs were surprisingly low, and my parents were all in favor of my going to the Quaker boarding school, so I would be away for a while from Rudi, who had a little attic room above my parents' apartment. Rudi thought it would be good for me to step back from my tight involvement with the family. I felt a great need to gain some distance from everyone and to have a chance to find myself. Given the long winter and spring breaks I spent at home, I was at the school for only seven months, but how I enjoyed the timeout from adult responsibilities! I read John Galsworthy's *Forsyte Saga* and Thomas Hardy's *Tess of the d'Urbervilles*, plus a great deal of English poetry. Soon, I was able to think in English and I became proficient enough in reading Latin to translate parts of Virgil's classic epic poem, the *Aeneid*.

The countryside was peaceful, and I did a great deal of walking, which was also restorative.

Love letters between Rudi and me went back and forth at least twice a week. His were full of longing for me, but they also contained information about his attempts to make concrete contacts for the future. He even sent an inquiry to Leopold Stokowski to find out what it would take to become a sound engineer in the field of classical music.

My letters to Rudi were no less loving than his, but while I looked forward to adult life at his side, I also intended to enjoy the next few months of "play time" at the Quaker school.

In December 1945, during winter break, Rudi and I became officially engaged. He had designed a little card showing a young man and a young woman meeting where two trails merge into one path, leading uphill to an attractive chalet in the mountains. The text read: "Together upward despite everything." We exchanged wedding-band-style gold rings and celebrated our engagement in my parents' apartment with our good neighbors of the war years, Rudi's cousin Ilse, and Anne-Marie, one of my school friends from the Jewish school, who had also survived Terezin. Later in the evening we were joined by another girlfriend from my first high school, Joyce van der Veen, who was well on her way to becoming a professional dancer. Food and drink were still rationed, so our fare was simple, but Mother sang *Lieder*, other guests recited poetry, and Joyce performed an exciting gypsy dance.

Although the Nuremberg Trials of the chief Nazi criminals must have been in full swing at that time, I do not remember that we focused on them. We were too busy healing from the terrible war years and trying to work toward a worthwhile future. Whenever I saw a reference to the trials in the newspaper, I reacted with impatience. *Why not just shoot those criminals*, I thought, a rash response of which I am not very proud.

~

In early fall of 1946, Rudi and I started life as university students. Rudi took his piano and his father's desk (both of which had been hidden with kindly neighbors) to the technical university at Delft, where he enrolled as a chemical engineering major. I registered at Amsterdam City University in the Department of Ethnography. We planned to spend every other weekend together, alternating between Delft and Amsterdam.

The first time I traveled to Delft, I carried along a hefty tome about the Peruvian Incas, fully determined to read not only on the train but also during most of the weekend. Little came of that as Rudi and I walked and talked a great deal and enjoyed holding each other.

When Rudi walked me back to the train station at the end of the weekend, he pointed to the new organic chemistry building and sighed wistfully: "It would be so much nicer if you joined me in my studies. You were always so good in science. Doing chemistry together would be so much more fun!"

I could see that he was lonesome, but I hesitated. I liked my courses in social studies. Moreover, it would be awkward for me to share Rudi's room in Delft. Living together as an unmarried couple would have been frowned upon. As a compromise, Rudi moved back to my family's home in Amsterdam, sending his desk and piano on a tow boat. We studied together at the Amsterdam City University, both majoring in chemistry with a minor in physics.

Rudi's aunt and uncle were not pleased that he had committed himself to his young girlfriend so early in life. In the summer of 1947, between our freshman and sophomore years, they invited him to Johannesburg, hoping to excite him about the possibilities of a new life with a secure income at his uncle's paint factory.

Rudi loved the great beauty of the country and the thrill of the Kruger Park, the huge game reserve in the South African Lowveld, where lions, elephants, and giraffes lived in the wild. However, as a person who had barely survived discrimination and vicious racism, he was appalled at South African society, with institutionalized apartheid just around the corner. Moving to Johannesburg was out of the question. His relatives were deeply disappointed, but they were generous enough to keep supporting Rudi with a monthly stipend until he finished school.

Once I reached the respectable age of twenty, we decided to get married. We loved each other deeply, and the hard times we had gone through together left no doubt that we wanted to share our lives for better and for worse, until death parted us. With Rudi's parents and so many close friends and relatives missing and our union long since consummated, we felt a big wedding would be out of place. We restricted ourselves to the least expensive formalities at Amsterdam City Hall, where we were one of three couples a civil servant married in a single session on the morning of October 15, 1947. Our marriage celebration was a subdued yet joyous affair. In a simple white dress, arms loaded with colorful dahlias, I said my vows as Rudi beamed. Otto Frank shared our happiness as our best man. Rudi's only remaining relative, Ilse, the cousin who had survived the concentration camps, represented his family at our wedding.

My parents treated the ten of us to a festive dinner at a restaurant called *De Vijf Vliegen* (The Five Flies), and that was the whole celebration. Rudi and I spent our honeymoon, a rainy weekend, in a small bed-and-breakfast outside the city. The following day found us back at the university doing lab work.

Two and a half years later we had our real honeymoon, trekking from one mountain cabin to the next in the Swiss Alps as members of the organization "Friends of Nature." It was a

Just married! Rudi and Hansje leaving City Hall, Otto Frank behind the glass panel

glorious vacation, even though we had so little money that we shared one egg for breakfast. The war years had taught us how to make do. The main thing was that we had survived. Both of us felt that we owed it to those who had been less lucky to make something positive out of our life together.

Chapter Twenty

RESTORATION

✣ ✣ ✣

While Rudi and I gradually found our bearings, Germany was struggling to reorient itself after the devastating war years. In 1949, seventy-three-year-old Konrad Adenauer, former mayor of the city of Cologne, was elected the first chancellor of the post–World War II Federal Republic of (West) Germany, the FRG (in German, *BRD* for *Bundesrepublik Deutschland*). A seasoned, strongly anti-communist leader dedicated to liberal democracy and Western-oriented foreign policy, Adenauer led West Germany to a position of economic strength, centrality in Western Europe, and international respect. After serving as chancellor for fourteen years, he resigned in 1963. By then, he was in his eighties and known affectionately by the nickname of *der Alte* (the old man).

When asked why so many officials, judges, and policemen with past Nazi affiliations were employed by the government and in the judiciary of the new republic, Adenauer quoted what he called "a bit of Rhenish wisdom": "It is not wise to throw out dirty water when there is no clean water to replace it." He considered denazification unworkable, judging it inexpedient to purge the new system of supporters of the old. Along with many other Germans, he believed the best policy was to bury the past and go forward. Under his extended leadership, West Germany pardoned itself and prospered.[1]

With this point of view predominating after the war, some German citizens reproached critics of the Nazis for "befouling their own nest." After all, prewar and postwar Germans were the same people. Jörg Friedrich put the matter succinctly in his 1984 book *Die kalte Amnestie* [the cold amnesty]: "The Federal Republic was an entity constructed under the compulsion of pleasing everybody. It was the fatherland of the Nazi people and of their enemies, of the persecutors and the persecuted. That tear in its fabric has stayed with it."[2]

Realizing that denazification was likely to remain half hearted and inconsistent, that it might prove to be destructive rather than constructive, Calmeyer turned away from the political arena. He had suffered under Hitler, but he knew that he had done some good, to the extent that circumstances permitted. Under the Allies and Adenauer, he felt he had failed.

Thomas Mann, one of Calmeyer's favorite writers, likewise despaired of his early hopes for social transformation. In 1942, he had written expectantly: "Germany will be cleansed of everything that had to do with the filth of Hitlerism and of anything that made it possible." In 1954, he had to concede: "Now it cannot be denied, that of the hopes of the year 1945 hardly a single one has been fulfilled."[3]

From 1953 on, former National Socialist district heads sat in the German parliament next to former concentration camp victims. A great many Nazi perpetrators went unpunished. Not until 1968 would there be a real change of power.

Starting in 1949, after the Federal Republic of Germany was admitted to the United Nations, Calmeyer became involved in UNESCO, the United Nations Education, Science, and Culture Organization, along with his Dutch friend Wim Verkade and his former coworker Heinrich Miessen. He traveled with Ruth or son Peter to France, Southern Germany, Switzerland, and Austria.[4]

Calmeyer's law office thrived. His early childhood neighbor and fellow lawyer Eberhard Westerkamp was a regular visitor. Eberhard never failed to deliver a blue cornflower on his friend's birthday, June 23. In Germany, the cornflower is a symbol from Romantic poetry, expressing the longing for a perfect world. Westerkamp deemed this the appropriate gift for Calmeyer, whom he considered "an incurable romantic."[5]

At the office, the secretary, Ruth Mnich, and Ines Hentschel had become friends. When they noticed a file with the puzzling title "Sourdough," they asked Calmeyer about this client. He explained that in the Sourdough file he collected possible "starters," ideas for initiatives to stimulate cultural activity in Osnabrück. In cooperation with the city's director of archives and other friends and acquaintances, he launched numerous projects that would enrich the cultural life of Osnabrück for years to come: academic weeks, bringing visiting professors from Münster, Göttingen, Groningen, Berlin, and other universities to give public lectures; a film club that grew into one of the largest in West Germany; piano recitals and play readings that evolved into stage performances; and a literary society, of which he served as president, while bookstore owner Heinrich Wenner pulled the necessary strings in the background.

People felt a great need to catch up with the world after twelve years of the Nazis' "blood and soil culture." Calmeyer introduced the people of Osnabrück to Faulkner, Hemingway,

Dos Passos, O'Neill, Camus, and Sartre. The latter's irreverent *Dirty Hands*, an intensely political melodrama of 1948, scandalized the local bishop. Calmeyer hoped that by giving his fellow citizens fresh food for thought, he might do more to cleanse the society of its Nazi past than he could through political activities.

Peter Calmeyer joined his father and Joker, Hans's beloved dachshund, on long Sunday walks in the countryside. Peter recalled that his father used the opportunities to deliver lectures, often on themes from Prussian or English history, subjects on which Peter excelled when he took his *Abitur*, the final high school examination.

Peter and his father also read Marx, Nietzsche, and Martin Heidegger, who had been an ardent Nazi. According to Peter, Calmeyer did not like the way Marx used language. Father and son found Nietzsche "stylistically brilliant," but neither believed a word he wrote. They relegated Heidegger's *Holzwege* (Off the Beaten Track; literal translation, "dead-end trails"), the philosopher's first postwar work, to the garbage can, a rare and devastating verdict coming from someone who loved books as much as Calmeyer did.[6]

At the end of 1949, a trial in Osnabrück dealt with the destruction of the local synagogue on *Kristallnacht*, the "Night of Broken Glass," the pogrom of November 9, 1938. Wilhelm Münzer, district head of the Nazi Party at the time, was one of four men charged. The accused maintained their innocence, testifying that spontaneous ignition must have caused the synagogue to burn down—unless the Jews themselves had committed arson. Witnesses at the trial were massively intimidated by threats from former Nazis. Proceedings had to be interrupted and continued at a secret location. Münzer's codefendants were sentenced to nine or ten months of incarceration, while Münzer himself was acquitted "in the name of the people."[7] Perhaps direct involvement on his part could not be proven. More likely, though, this was one of the many cases illustrating the German saying: "The little guys are hanged; the big shots go free!" Calmeyer must have swallowed hard!

Except for his wife, his son, and Eberhard Westerkamp, no one in Osnabrück knew about Calmeyer's rescue operation in the Netherlands. Most people would have taken his actions amiss. As late as 1963, Calmeyer confided to the Dutch newspaper *Algemeen Dagblad*: "To have been anti-Nazi is no recommendation for a West German lawyer."[8]

Guests who stayed with the Calmeyers at Friedrichstrasse 48 in the early fifties, among them Hans's "niece" Caroline Redlich and her brother Thomas, remembered the upstairs room, comfortably furnished in the appealing *Biedermeier* style of the 1830s, where "Uncle Hans" had set up his tin soldiers. They described him as sensitive, cultivated, and excitable.

Thomas, who was twelve or thirteen years old at the time, recalled:

> Hans Calmeyer took me seriously and talked to me the way he would to an adult. A very well-balanced and friendly person. He would come up to people in a charismatic sort of way, but never tried to dominate them. Yes, and then there was Ines, . . . [a] beautiful young woman, whom I liked very much. I did not notice, then, that possibly a love affair was already going on between her and the head of the family. However, in the light of my present experience of life, I am aware of a powerfully sensual aura in the

Calmeyer houschold. The cerebral pair, Ruth and Peter, were not up to that.[9]

Hans Calmeyer and Ruth's niece, Ines, were, indeed, strongly drawn to each other. Ines became pregnant in 1952. She and Hans wanted to have their love child. Ruth demanded that the child be aborted, and Peter, eager to avoid scandal, supported his mother. But Calmeyer resisted their pressures. To bear the child, Ines moved to Goslar, a town about 150 miles east of Osnabrück, where her mother lived. Hans Calmeyer's second son, Michael, was born there on February 17, 1953.

Chapter Twenty-one

Embracing New Life

✤ ✤ ✤

Rudi and I also added to the postwar baby boom. Four months after we got married, I became pregnant, although we had not really planned to start a family before finishing our studies.

No one was more delighted about our news than my father, who at age sixty was ready for a grandchild. Since Rudi and I— and my entire family—were still stateless, my father suggested that I give birth to the baby in England. Our child would be born a British citizen, so at least one member of our family would have a nationality. Since the British National Health Service was just getting established, expenses would be minimal.

A cousin of Rudi's mother as well as my mother's best friend, Alice Koppel, lived in London. Both made me welcome, but since I had known "Aunt Alice" from early childhood in Frankfurt, I stayed mostly with the Koppels.

Their house was in Finchley, in the northern part of London. Shortly after my arrival, the Koppels arranged for me to meet a physician friend who connected me to Redhill Hospital in Edgware. On my twenty-first birthday I was accepted there as a future patient. The file clerk was baffled when I answered her standard questions: Nationality? Without. Religion? Without. Luckily, I had an address: that of the Koppels.

I felt at home there. Mother had visited them in Nelson, near Manchester, in the summer of 1939, just before the outbreak of the war, when Alice was pregnant. Her only child, Edward James Martin, "Ted" for short, was born there in February 1940. He and I hit it off particularly well when I stayed at the Koppels' in the summer and early fall of 1948. I remember playing a little game with him on the cement slab that led to their modest back garden. You had to bounce a seven- or eight-inch rubber ball, turn around, and do all kinds of other tricks while reciting: "Oliver Twist / Can you do this? / If so, do so."

I helped in the house as much as I could, and I tried to learn some kitchen skills from Alice, who was an excellent cook. When not needed, I explored the sights of the city, such as the House of Parliament and Buckingham Palace. I walked across the Tower Bridge and visited the British Museum, the National and the Tate Galleries, and Kew Gardens. Soon, I learned to travel the Tube like a Londoner. At night, I knitted for the baby. I longed for Rudi's company, but we could not afford for him to come over. Instead, he was using all his spare time to remake our attic rooms into a cozy little apartment for the three of us, and in his frequent letters he kept me informed about his progress.

Giving birth did not worry me; it was, after all, a most natural occurrence. Our baby boy was born without any complications on October 6, 1948. When Rudi welcomed us back home at Schiphol, the Amsterdam airport, Ralph was thirteen days old and had a British passport, albeit without a picture. After the terrible experiences we had gone through, we were confident that we were launching him into a better future. War was a thing of the past; the United Nations would see to that!

I did not go back to the university, but rather filled a part-time opening as an X-ray technician so we were not totally financially dependent on Rudi's relatives and my parents. Rudi soon became a graduate assistant in a nuclear physics lab and grew rightly concerned about the radiation I was exposed to as an X-ray technician, especially since we didn't want Ralph to grow up as an only child.

While our second baby was on its way, my parents, my sisters, and Rudi and I, at long last, acquired Dutch citizenship. The normal cost of naturalization was the equivalent of US $50 at the time. This fee was waived in Rudi's case because he had helped the Dutch underground during the war by providing the authentic German document needed to pass the border from western Belgium to the Netherlands. He bought a secondhand Rolleiflex with the welcome windfall. That camera recorded our lives over many decades, especially our travels.

Our second son, Fred, was born a Netherlander on June 4, 1952. It was wonderful to have Rudi nearby this time. The four of us still lived on the attic floor above my parents' Amsterdam apartment and shared their bathroom, but we had our own kitchen upstairs. My father had reestablished himself in the notions business. Susi, my older sister, worked in my father's office and also took some classes in political science at the City University. Marion, our youngest sister, majored in French at the same school. I divided my time between taking care of the two boys and typing Rudi's doctoral dissertation on a topic of experimental nuclear physics. He had written it in English so it would be accessible to his peers abroad. Rudi defended his dissertation in December 1954 in a public ceremony, as Dutch tradition has it. Besides the family, all our friends and wartime relations attended the event. Only Otto Frank was missing. He had married Elfriede Geiringer, another survivor of the death camps, a year before, and the couple had moved to Basel, Switzerland. We stayed in touch, but it would be many years before we would see each other again.

Immediately after Rudi acquired his PhD, we started our *Wanderjahre*, our years of travel. Rudi won a UNESCO scholarship that took us to Liverpool, England, for the first half of 1955. The winter was bitter cold, but it was exciting to live abroad as a family. Son Ralph bravely went to first grade in an English elementary school. For me, one of the highlights was hosting my parents and driving with them and the children to the beautiful Lake District.

Our next adventure took us by Holland-America Line passenger ship to the United States. Rudi had been invited for a year as a postdoctoral fellow at Indiana University. We landed in Hoboken, New Jersey, and were overwhelmed by the many cars and the huge skyscrapers of New York, where we stopped over to link up with friends of our parents, including the Koppels. They had moved to an attractive apartment at Central Park West when Ted was thirteen.

From New York we took the train to Bloomington, Indiana. The night we arrived, our next-door neighbor Jenny offered us her car keys so we could go shopping. Neither Rudi nor I knew how to maneuver her huge automatic Buick, so Jenny, although quite pregnant, kindly took us to an enormous supermarket. Coming from a country with small neighborhood stores and an economy of scarcity, I was so overwhelmed by the seemingly endless aisles of well-stocked shelves that I burst into tears.

Several neighbors in our married-student housing compound, all young families with husbands studying under the GI

Bill, were incredibly helpful and made us feel quite welcome. Our boys found plenty of playmates, and the oldest fit right into second grade. Rudi's research was well appreciated, and I was able to take two American literature classes at Indiana University. I remember reading Herman Melville's *Moby Dick* and Robert Penn Warren's *All the King's Men*. Both Rudi and I greatly appreciated the performances at the excellent IU Music Department. I still find myself humming tunes from our first American musical, *South Pacific*.

What we missed were in-depth conversations. No one asked how we had survived the war, which seemed so far from the American shores. We soon learned that all people wanted to hear was how much we liked living in the United States.

A week before Christmas, a letter came from my older sister. Since Mother had always been the family correspondent, I opened Susi's letter with misgivings. They were justified. Susi informed us of my father's sudden death following a heart attack. We knew he'd had some heart problems, but they hadn't seemed serious when we'd left the Netherlands in September. I felt quite bereft. Father was only sixty-eight, and I suddenly realized how many things I wanted to ask him. Now I would not have the chance! The boys would greatly miss their grandfather, especially little Fred, who, when asked what he wanted to be when he grew up had answered, "I want to be a grandpa!"

While living in Bloomington, we were able to do some traveling. Thanks to an exchange babysitting arrangement with a neighbor couple, I was able to join Rudi when he went to a conference in Washington, DC. I was impressed by the Capitol and the Lincoln Memorial, and I spent hours at the Smithsonian. What tickled me greatly were the signs on dioramas featuring Native American life before the late 1800s. They were labeled "pre-historic"!

At the end of the school year, the four of us took a road trip across the Rocky Mountains, where we went to an honest-to-goodness rodeo, and on to several of the great American national parks, including the stupendous Grand Canyon, the Hopi cliff dwellings of Mesa Verde, and the amazing rock formations of Bryce Canyon and Zion. With no plans to return to the United States after our year abroad ended, we thought we had better take the opportunity to see it all, despite the fact that I was pregnant again. The huge distances staggered us, and we kept marveling at the stamina of the first settlers as they traversed the roadless expanse with their covered wagons.

Soon the year was over, and we had to go back to Europe. It was hard to return to Amsterdam with my father no longer there to welcome us. Mother, twelve years younger than he, had adjusted most admirably. She was eager to join us at our next post: Geneva, Switzerland, where Rudi had a one-year research appointment at CERN, the European Center for Nuclear Research.

Ralph, now a third grader, again adapted surprisingly well. He went to a local school and, with some help from me, picked up French almost as quickly as he had learned English. Rudi rubbed shoulders with colleagues from a dozen European countries, the best in his field. His research was exciting.

On December 17, 1956, our daughter Elka was born. After two boys, we were overjoyed to have a little girl. My mother stayed with us for many months to help out. She loved the Alps with their beautiful, fragrant meadows as much as we did, and joined us on numerous weekend outings.

The location and the international atmosphere of Geneva suited us well, but the Swiss were not nearly as forthcoming as our former American neighbors had been. We were considered *étrangers,* foreigners, tolerated but certainly not to be integrated into Swiss society. Moreover, appointments at CERN were typically temporary. Researchers were expected to return to their home institution after one or two years. Rudi had no home institution. Although he certainly could have found a position in the Netherlands, he was not sure he wanted one, since his Dutch colleagues tended to make him self-conscious about his slight German accent. He was afraid that he would always be considered an outsider.

I can still see Rudi and me, thoroughly weighing our options as we paced up and down the long, tree-lined drive that led to a commanding manor house. We lived on the estate, in what was formerly the gardener's cottage. Our sons had been happy in the United States. At the time, people there seemed to be more tolerant of foreign accents than in the more homogeneous European countries. What if we settled there?

My mother was horrified by the idea that we might move to the U.S. for good. She had relatives in the States who had written to her about pervasive racism and deplorable anti-Semitism. Moreover, she had a strong aversion to unbridled capitalism. The latter, we assured her, was a thing of the past ever since President Franklin Delano Roosevelt's New Deal. After much hesitation, Rudi accepted an assistant professorship at the University of California in Davis.

Getting our immigration visas in 1957 was easy. In the year of *Sputnik*, the United States was eager to welcome a young nuclear physicist to strengthen the country's scientific ranks. We could not help but remember that twenty years earlier, when Rudi was just one more refugee trying to flee Europe for his life, there was no way for him and his parents to acquire the coveted visas. We were the same people, but the circumstances had drastically changed.

Rudi went ahead to Davis in September 1957, while Mother and I took the children back to Amsterdam to organize our move and pack our belongings. Both boys went to the Montessori school around the corner, the same school Anne Frank had attended until 1941. It now proudly bears her name. We were still in Amsterdam when my grandmother, fiercely independent Omi, died, after a brief bout with pneumonia. As a professional singer, she had been an early career woman. If it had not been for her and Hans Calmeyer, we would not have been alive. Omi had lived to be eighty-nine, and now she deserved to rest in peace.

Chapter Twenty-two

THE WORLD IS OPEN

✣ ✣ ✣

In early November 1957, I flew with the three children to San Francisco, a long journey with a transfer in London from one airport to another and then a fueling stop at Frobisher Bay on Baffin Island. I still remember the huge snow tunnel through which we had to walk to get to the reception hall.

It was a pleasure to live in the small college town of Davis, California. We could get around by bicycle, and I was able to enroll in a few classes. By that time, physics was no longer an option for me. The long lab hours would be hard to reconcile with looking after our children, and strong nepotism policies would make it impossible for me to work in the same department as my husband. My original field of social sciences lost its attraction when I saw the super-sized textbooks. Instead I capitalized on my foreign-language skills and majored in German with a minor in French. I also changed my first name from Hannelore (too Germanic) and the Dutch diminutive Hansje (unpronounceable) to Laureen.

Alas, it turned out that Davis was not the right fit for us. Rudi was not happy in a very competitive, rather than cooperative, department, and the summers in California's central valley proved much too hot for us. After two years, we moved to Portland, Oregon, a great city for raising a family. We did not mind the rain, since we had brought our webfeet from Amsterdam. Rudi became an associate professor at what was then Portland State College (now Portland State University), and I graduated there at the end of spring term 1962. A week later the school's intensive summer program had an overflowing first-year German class, and I was asked to teach a section. I accepted with some trepidation but found that I greatly enjoyed teaching.

Despite Mother's strong misgivings about the United States, she applied for an immigration visa too. She gave up the Amsterdam apartment where the family had lived since April 1936 and joined us in Portland. Henceforth, Mother divided her time evenly between my sisters in Europe and us, the "American branch" of the family, and for several years the only one with children. Both of my sisters were single when we left Europe. Susi married soon thereafter and started a family in 1961. Marion became a multilingual translator for the European Community in Luxembourg, married late, and never had children.

For fourteen years, Mother's room, furnished with Omi's charming *Biedermeier* furniture, was the jewel of our house in Portland's West Hills. We had found our niche and felt accepted even without learning to relish fast food or becoming baseball or football fans. Since I had good memories of my Quaker teachers at the Ommen boarding school, I attended Friends' meeting for a number of years, and the children went to a Quaker Sunday school. Rudi came along occasionally, but more often than not he met his spiritual needs by playing his piano on Sunday mornings. Neither one of us felt the urge to practice Judaism and raise the children as Jews.

We would have been happy in the beautiful Pacific Northwest were it not for the escalating Cold War tensions. In 1962, the United States started stationing nuclear weapons on German soil and allowed the West German government input into their maintenance. Rudi and I joined protest demonstrations under the banner "No German Finger on the Nuclear Trigger." After what we had gone through, we didn't want to see Germany rearmed. One of Rudi's colleagues spotted us among the demonstrators and asked the next day with a smirk: "How can you join a demonstration? You're not even citizens!" That could be remedied, we retorted, and we immediately applied for citizenship.

Early in 1963, we affirmed our allegiance to the United States, though we testified that we would not bear arms to defend the country, because that would violate our pacifist convictions. I was heading the Quaker Sunday school that year, which convinced the judge that our conscientious objections were sincere. Our two sons, fourteen and ten at the time, confirmed that they had been raised as war resisters. I joined the Women's International League for Peace and Freedom and engaged for many years in intensive antiwar leafletting. As a survivor of World War II, I knew that wars are a bane for mankind. Mother treasured her Dutch passport and felt no need to apply for United States citizenship.

Time and again, I was invited to teach German classes at Portland State University and one year also at Reed College. I enjoyed teaching and found it rewarding. When Rudi took his first sabbatical at the University of Washington in 1965–1966, I jumped at the opportunity to acquire a master's degree there.

By 1968 we had finally saved enough money to return to Europe for the first time in eleven years. Rudi was invited for the academic year to do research at the University of Groningen in the Netherlands, and I was eager to show the younger children where they had come from. Since we often spoke Dutch at home, especially while Mother was with us, they knew that language reasonably well. Fred went to tenth grade and Elka to

The Nussbaum family, including Laureen's mother in front of their Portland house, 1966

sixth. Ralph was off to college at the University of Oregon, but he managed to arrange for a junior year exchange program in Stuttgart, Germany.

Elka, who considered World War II ancient history, was amazed to find how much the war years were still on people's minds in the Netherlands. It wasn't just her parents who kept referring back to the war; almost all of the middle-aged and older people we met in Groningen did. In addition, there were many monuments recalling atrocities and bravery during the occupation years. Our sixth grader adapted so well to her Dutch surroundings that when Carol, Ralph's fiancée, visited in June of 1969 and Elka could not hold her own in an English conversation, she burst out in exasperation, "You just wait till my English better gets!" In my subsequent teaching, I have often used Elka's outburst to demonstrate to my students that the word order of German and Dutch can be mastered within one year!

Now that we were back in Europe, Rudi and I felt the need to confront ourselves with Germany, our native country. We drove from Hamburg in the north to Munich in the south and on into Austria, stopping at Bergen-Belsen with its mounds of mass graves, the last resting place of Rudi's mother and the Frank girls. The camp where tens of thousands had suffered and died was eerily peaceful under a light snow cover. We visited Dachau, and finally Mauthausen. There we stared aghast at the notorious stone quarry where our friend Rolf and so many others had met their deaths. Ralph accompanied us for most of that trip. Emotionally, all these years, German had remained the language of the enemy for Rudi and me. We felt a lingering, irrational reluctance to speak it in public. Hence, it was a real breakthrough for Rudi when he persuaded himself to give his guest lectures in German rather than in English.

Most of our Dutch friends lived in or around Amsterdam. They used our stay in Groningen to visit that "faraway" city for the first time. We smiled. Coming from the United States, we no longer considered a three-hour car or train ride a long trip. Mother brought Susi's oldest child, Ronald, who at age seven was a fine guest. Susi gave birth to her second daughter while we were in the Netherlands. In July 1969, my youngest sister, Marion, arranged a joyful celebration of Mother's seventieth birthday in charming Luxembourg.

En route to the Swiss Alps, we visited Otto Frank and his wife "Fritzi" (Elfriede) in Basel. We told them that we had been impressed by an exhibit at the Anne Frank House in Amsterdam, where images of the horrors of the My Lai massacre in Vietnam had been displayed alongside those of the atrocities in the concentration camps. Otto objected to the juxtaposition because he felt that we owed the Americans gratitude rather than criticism. Rudi and I dropped the subject and asked him instead to show us his bookshelves with copies of Anne's *Diary* translated into some fifty-five languages.

An octogenarian now, Otto spent most of his days answering letters from children and teenagers all over the world. Being in contact with young people who had read the diary linked him to his daughters. We reported that our Portland circles of friends and acquaintances showed only limited interest in how we had survived World War II. The name Anne Frank was, however, slowly penetrating to the American public, grace to the movie released in 1959 that won an Academy Award for Shelley Winters.

Our return to the United States in the autumn of 1969 was profoundly unsettling. The Vietnam War was escalating, and opposition voices were drowned out. We could now see how hard it must have been for German anti-Nazis to swim against the current in the mid-1930s. All of us had a hard time readjusting. Ralph became quite radicalized; he and Carol, recently wed in a lovely Quaker ceremony, even spent a few days in a Eugene, Oregon, jail. I found solace in studying for my PhD, a long-term project since I had to commute to Seattle while teaching part time at Portland State University.

After Fred left home for the Massachusetts Institute of Technology (MIT), Rudi negotiated a personal exchange with a New Zealand colleague at the University of Canterbury in Christchurch, New Zealand. Elka and I traveled with him. From September 1971 to early March 1972, we spent a fascinating time down under, stopping in Tahiti, Samoa, and Fiji on the way out and in Australia, Indonesia, Malaysia, and Japan on the way back. In most of these countries, Rudi gave one or more lectures about his research, which made us feel like visitors rather than tourists. Everywhere we went, our hosts arranged for our lodging and showed us around.

In New Zealand, we explored the subtropical North Island, with its remnants of native Maori culture. Closer to our temporary Christchurch home, we crossed the Southern Alps on foot. After a presentation in Brisbane, we snorkeled at the Great Barrier Reef among schools of colorful exotic fish. Then, on the way to the Indonesian University in Bandung we stopped for a few days on the island of Bali, with its rich Hindu culture, and subsequently crossed over to Java, where we visited the Borobudur, the ancient Buddhist temple with its many statues of the meditating Buddha in *stupas*, bell-shaped towers pointing to heaven. In Japan, our host took us to the Imperial Gardens in Kyoto, created more than three centuries ago. Not in our wildest dreams during the years 1940–1945 did we ever envision traveling the Pacific Rim with its many different cultures.

For our second-to-last stop homebound in Kuala Lumpur, Malaysia, Rudi had scheduled a presentation at the Chinese University there. Our visit coincided with President Nixon's famous trip to China, so our hosts treated us to a replica of Nixon's multicourse dinner in Beijing, including suckling pig. We felt honored, but more importantly, we experienced relief that the war in Vietnam would soon be over.

In 1974, I finally passed my qualifying exams at the University of Washington. It took me another two years to complete my dissertation, a substantial volume on the female figures in the work of the progressive German poet-playwright Bertolt Brecht. Over a period of thirty-five years, the women in Brecht's work evolved from sweethearts and prostitutes to formidable mother figures, courageous, resilient, and life sustaining. Having lived through the German occupation, foraged for food, supported friends in hiding, and been aware of the misery in which people dear to me died, I felt a special affinity with Brecht's Shen Te (*The Good Person of Szechwan*) and Grusha (*The Caucasian*

Chalk Circle), for their resourcefulness, grit, and resilience. Yet, these qualities would not have saved Grusha's little boy without the decision of Judge Azdak, a maverick figure akin to Hans Calmeyer, as I would learn later.

On the day I defended my dissertation, our daughter, Elka, presented me with a small quilt. Using her pink baby blanket for the lining and a piece of flannel as the backing, she'd composed a diamond pattern from scraps I had saved. In the middle of the quilt she had embroidered, "My Mother Figure," and in the four corners, the words "Robust," "Resourceful," "Resilient," and "Practical." I was deeply touched by this meaningful gift, and even now, forty years later, I won't consider taking a little nap without Elka's quilt.

Chapter Twenty-three

SLIGHTLY ECCENTRIC

✥ ✥ ✥

Since childhood, Hans Calmeyer had identified with "Lucky Hans," the main character in a popular Grimm's fairy tale. Good-natured, kindhearted Hans is a naïve and honest man unconcerned with possessions and easily exploited by others. After working hard for seven years, he wants to go home to see his mother. His master pays him with a lump of gold.

Hans sets off carrying the bulky nugget but meets a traveler riding on horseback and exchanges his heavy gold for the swift horse. The horse bucks him off, and he trades his horse for a cow to enjoy her milk. Then he trades his cow for a pig, his pig for a goose, his goose for a heavy grindstone. When Hans quenches his thirst at a well, the grindstone falls in and sinks to the bottom. Hans exclaims, "No one under the sun is as lucky as I am!" With a light heart, free of any burden, he walks on to his mother's home.

Calmeyer, too, had always felt lucky. For much of his life he was able to look on the bright side, and his penchant for enthusiasm often overruled a more circumspect view. However, where fairy-tale Hans felt no need to reproach himself, Hans Calmeyer was burdened with regrets in later years. Not least among them were memories of the "unburied," the victims of the Holocaust he had been unable to save.

We do not know what went on in his mind regarding his extra-marital affair and his illegitimate son. Michael recalled in 2015: "My mother and father decided not to allow Ruth to demand my abortion, which is why my mother literally fled back to my grand-mother and bore me in Goslar, far from [Ruth's] very demanding reach. She was known throughout the family (not just our little side) as 'Die Katze' (the Cat)."[1]

Calmeyer's good friend Fritz Harbsmeyer, a local business-man, voiced his hope that Hans would at long last give up on his marriage to Ruth in order to marry Ines and pursue the erotic and emotional fulfillment that life with her offered.[2] But it was not to be. In 1955, Ruth fell down the stairs and broke the base of her skull, a major injury. That accident may have been decisive. Calmeyer had made a commitment to his wife and would not shirk his responsibilities.[3]

Calmeyer said of himself, "a knight, not a saint; that is what I was striving for."[4] Though he was not a perfect man, he could be trusted to act on his convictions. Lovely Ines was an irresistible temptation, but she knew from the start of the affair that Hans was bound to Ruth by vows he would never repudiate.

Ines found a job working in the office of Hans Har-borth, the bishop of the Goslar-area Lutheran church as well as Michael's state-appointed guardian. She and young Michael lived in picturesque Goslar for a little over ten years. Calmeyer visited when he could.

Hans Calmeyer with his son Michael and Michael's mother, Ines, 1957

Hans would arrive in his Volkswagen Beetle with Joker, to his young son's delight. Calmeyer's secretary Ruth Mnich usually came along. She and Ines remained close friends. For years, Ruth Mnich served as a courier between Calmeyer and Ines, who raised Michael alone. She had the help of a small monthly child-support check Harborth had ordered. Ruth Calmeyer, in her capacity as her husband's business manager, reluctantly wrote the checks.

On his website, Michael wrote:

> Every son needs a father, and to differing degrees some fathers are everpresent and many are not. Michael only was able to see Hans Calmeyer once or twice a year in his ten years growing up in Goslar, Germany, but he was unaware as a child that this was unusual, and those few visits . . . were as loving a father-child relationship as could ever be imagined.

Calmeyer sometimes sent Michael copies of his poems, but otherwise they had little communication.

In 1963, Ines took Michael and her mother to the United States and settled in Evanston, Illinois, near Chicago, where an older sister lived. She found a job in the library of Northwestern University.[5] Her mother died from a brain tumor less than a year later, leaving Ines to raise Michael on her own. Since Peter Calmeyer destroyed all papers relating to his father's other family, we have no way of telling how Hans Calmeyer related to Ines and Michael, once mother and son had left for the United States.

Just before departing for America, Michael spent a week in the Calmeyer household. "Even then," Michael recalled, "Ruth threatened to enter a mental hospital, which she threatened and sometimes did every time Hans wanted to visit me and my mother. . . , which he managed nevertheless to do about once a year, against all odds, with her knowledge."

Eberhard Westerkamp ascribed "eccentric inclinations" to Hans Calmeyer; Heino Haarmann, a fellow lawyer, remarked on his "bohemian streak." Neither friends nor colleagues were surprised when Calmeyer's reading frenzies led him onto shaky ground. For instance, while immersed in the work of Justus Möser, the prominent eighteenth-century jurist and social theorist from Osnabrück, Calmeyer read about the *Sassen* (in standard German "*Sachsen*," for "Saxons") of northern Germany. Calmeyer believed these people were not Saxons but rather Celts, and that he himself was their descendant. The teetotaler began to think of himself as an "ever-inebriated Irishman." He also collected what he thought were Celtic words, those starting with "kn": *knave, knickknack, knight, knoll, knot.* One of his "nieces" went so far as to suggest he change his name to "Knallmeyer," but he was not amused.[6]

❧

In 1953, Calmeyer became the legal adviser of the Dresdner Bank and moved his law office to Möserstrasse 7, to the second floor above a branch office. His legal career prospered in the rapidly expanding postwar economy.

In subsequent years, Calmeyer carried on his office life much as before. The six or seven ladies on his staff, from Ruth Mnich down to the file clerk, were devoted to him. One employee looked after the daily supply of cigarettes: ten boxes of Ecuadors, five for Ruth and five for Hans. He was almost as dependent on coffee as on cigarettes.[7]

Calmeyer liked to dictate directly to his typists while walking to and fro. He remembered statements verbatim, specifying each comma and period. If the typists made a mistake, he patiently corrected it, radiating warmth and kindness with a gentle authority. His laughter was hearty. According to Gerald Bruns, the young son of a client, he had, "a way of caressing you without touching."[8]

When he won a case, Calmeyer would bring each member of the staff a small bouquet of violets. As son Michael put it, "My business-sense-free father . . . just wanted to do good for his clients and never bothered to charge them himself."

Ruth handled the billing and tried to make sure her husband was not victimized. Despite his wife's protectiveness, he continued to promise some clients free legal advice. Ruth scolded and scoffed: "It would have been better if my husband had become a pastor." Once, when Calmeyer represented Sinti (Gypsy) clients at no charge, they placed a live goose on his desk as a Christmas gift.[9]

Calmeyer valued general education. When hiring a new employee, he subjected each candidate to a little test: "Would you please name the countries surrounding the Mediterranean?" or "Can you tell me where Constantinople is located?" He liked to discuss even tricky legal problems with his office workers, and he accepted prospective lawyers as interns only after checking with the staff: "Shall we take him?"[10]

His employees could count on a ride home, especially when they worked late. Occasionally, Calmeyer took a group from the office to late-night film screenings. What he wanted from them was a critical view, always a critical view. When a valued staff member left the office, Calmeyer once said, "For me, it is as if I were losing a daughter."[11]

For the most part, Calmeyer did not use the familiar German *du* to address his employees, nor the formal *Sie*. Instead he spoke to them in the third person, an eighteenth-century style of address he may have picked up from his avid play-reading: "Linde, she did that very well!" he would say, or "Monika, has she learned the new waltz?" This quirk of speech added to his eccentricity.

Only with Ruth Mnich in the early postwar period and with a later senior employee, Brigitte Franz, did he use the familiar *du*.[12] In a melancholy moment, he confided to Brigitte that what he would really like to do was to sit on the ridge of a roof in the town of Halle, just northwest of Leipzig in East Germany— an odd choice at the time—and write poetry. Alternatively, he would love to take a suitcase full of books and withdraw to a lakeside cottage.[13]

As the years passed, Hans Calmeyer turned more and more inward. On his desk, next to a big ashtray and a cup of coffee, he stacked books of poetry, along with newspapers and magazines. Many legal colleagues, especially those with Nazi pasts, avoided contact with Calmeyer. Maintaining his inexorable sense of personal integrity, he would not deal with fellow lawyers or with clients he suspected of lying to him or misrepresenting their histories. The local judges appreciated Calmeyer's professional prowess. Alfred Emmerlich, president of the Osnabrück district court, said of him: "What he says and presents is very much to the point. There is no swagger. One likes to concentrate on his arguments and to follow them."[14]

Hans Calmeyer's wartime past as head of the office that decided the fate of Jews petitioning to be declared "Aryans" erupted into his postwar present at the time of the Eichmann trial in 1961. From the earliest years of the Hitler regime, Adolf Eichmann had been charged with removal of the Jews, which evolved from attempts to "stimulate emigration" to the long lines of cattle cars carrying European Jewry to the annihilation camps. A mild-mannered, even obsequious man with a receding hairline, Eichmann was the master logician of the so-called "final solution," a model of murderous efficiency.

At the end of the war in 1945, Eichmann went into hiding, first in Europe and eventually in Argentina, which he reached via the infamous "rat line" that helped many Nazis escape judgment. There he held a succession of jobs. Eichmann liked to refer to himself as an "emigration specialist." His wife and three sons joined him in Buenos Aires in 1952.

In 1960, the Mossad, Israel's intelligence service, tracked him down and verified his identity. One evening as Eichmann (using the alias Ricardo Klement) walked home from his usual bus stop, a four-man Mossad "snatch squad" pounced on him and threw him to the floor of their car. Nine days later, heavily sedated and supported by two Israeli agents—all three men dressed in El Al flight-attendant uniforms—Mossad flew him from Argentina to Jerusalem, where he stood trial in 1961.

Prosecutors presented their case over fifty-six days. More than a hundred people, including many Holocaust survivors, bore scaring witness to the atrocities of the Nazis' "final solution." Eichmann's defense was that he believed the Führer's words had the power of law, that he held a low rank in the Nazi hierarchy, and that he had merely followed orders. He was convicted of all fifteen charges brought against him for crimes against humanity and against the Jewish people and sentenced to death by hanging. At midnight June 1, 1962, he was executed.

Eichmann's trial, televised and widely reported in the media, sparked renewed interest in the Holocaust around the world. Simon Wiesenthal, who had played a role in locating the wily Eichmann, commented in his 1988 book *Justice, Not Vengeance*: "The world now understands the concept of 'desk murderer.' We know that one doesn't need to be fanatical, sadistic, or mentally ill to murder millions, that it is enough to be a loyal follower eager to do one's duty."[15]

On May 6, 1963, in the wake of the Eichmann trial, NWDR (*Nordwestdeutscher Rundfunk*), the German Northwest Broadcasting System, devoted most of its political journal *Panorama* to the white-collar perpetrators of World War II in The Hague. The program focused particularly on the activities of Dr. Erich Rajakowitsch. Among those who had their say were Dr. Louis de Jong of the Dutch Institute for War Documentation and Simon Wiesenthal, himself a Jewish concentration camp survivor. Hans Calmeyer appeared briefly, unfortunately introduced as "a former higher SS official." He was asked in the interview whether the upper echelon in the Office of the Reich Commissar in The Hague had known what the "final solution" entailed. Calmeyer answered with an unqualified, "Yes."[16]

Panorama apologized for the grievous mistake of misintroducing Hans Calmeyer, published a rectification, and paid him a compensation for suffering caused. All the same, Calmeyer was deeply shaken.[17]

One week later, Calmeyer had to appear as a witness at a Dutch police office in Oldenzaal, close to the German border. His law partner, Rolf Gurland, came along and chronicled Calmeyer's complete testimony in a tape recording. At the beginning of the session, Calmeyer sounds tense and strained. Dutch police officer Thijs Taconis was well prepared. He showed his witness a series of photos and documents.

Surprisingly, Calmeyer did not remember Rajakowitsch, his keenest antagonist during his early years in The Hague. Rajakowitsch had headed SR-J (*Sonderreferat Juden*), the Special Section for Jewish Affairs that later became Eichmann's Department IV B 4. Perhaps Calmeyer had never seen the SS man in uniform or had incorrectly deemed him "small fry."

As the conversation continued, Calmeyer appeared to relax. He took the view that subordinate German Nazi officers were to a large degree responsible for anti-Jewish agitation in the Netherlands, because they thought it would help to advance their careers. Rajakowitsch was sentenced to several years in a Vienna prison.[18]

Chapter Twenty-four

TOO LITTLE, TOO LITTLE!

✤ ✤ ✤

Hans Calmeyer turned sixty on Sunday, June 23, 1963. Any celebration was probably low key. The same year, architects inventoried the historical buildings in Osnabrück's city center with an eye to restoration. Also, in 1963, the city awarded the Möser medal, its most prestigious honor, to its son Erich

Hans Calmeyer in the early 1960s

Maria Remarque, whose antiwar novel *Im Westen nichts Neues* (*All Quiet on the Western Front,* 1929) Calmeyer had long considered a masterpiece. (Joseph Goebbels, the chief Nazi propagandist, had denounced the 1930 Hollywood film based on Remarque's book as a "Jewish piece of obscenity." When in 1930, the movie was first released in Germany, Nazi agitators smuggled mice and stink bombs into movie houses to stage "pressure from the street.")[1]

In 1963, one in four West Germans still considered the July 20, 1944, plot against Hitler's life an act of treason. The majority of high government officials and law professors of the Nazi state had retained their positions of authority. Calmeyer and his friend Fritz Harbsmeyer, regular readers of the progressive weekly *Der Spiegel*, deplored what they saw as West Germany's sure slide to the right.[2]

Meanwhile, in the Netherlands, the historian Dr. Jacob Presser had been tasked with writing the history of the destruction of Dutch Jewry during the German occupation. His monumental chronicle *Ondergang* (Destruction) was published in two volumes in 1965. The slightly abridged English translation in one volume, *Ashes in the Wind: The Destruction of Dutch Jewry,* came out in 1968. Calmeyer read the Dutch original fresh from the press and felt compelled to write to Presser immediately after his first perusal.

Presser was touched and called Calmeyer's letter *"een geweldig document, inderdaad"* (a formidable document, indeed). In his second volume of *Ondergang* he had devoted a whole chapter to Hans Calmeyer and he also mentioned him numerous times elsewhere in his chronicle. The historian had unequivocal praise for Calmeyer's rescue mission. In Presser's opinion, had a different person served in Calmeyer's position during the years 1941–1945 (not necessarily a convinced Nazi, but just a "normal," dutiful German official), many more Jews from the Netherlands would have died.[3] Fortunately, the correspondence has been preserved.

Osnabrück, September 27, 1965

Dear Dr. Presser!

My archaeologist son, Peter, returned last night from a visit to Leiden with the two volumes of *Ondergang*, for which I was already prepared by a review in the weekly *Die Zeit*. With burning interest, I have been reading all night in these two volumes. In doing so, my interest was hardly focused on my share in the suffering and guilt. Your theme, which you rightly call the *Ondergang*, has held me in its stranglehold since 1941. To this day, I have not been able to come to grips with myself, even less with the guilt and sense of failure all of us share. Hence, it is comforting to glean from your work that the same holds true for others, including yourself. At one point in volume two you ask yourself, the historian: "Are we now finished with it?"

No, we certainly are not finished with what happened and with our part in what happened, whether we were actors or sufferers. You rightly recognize that any action fell short, if it was not downright criminal. The well-intentioned contemporary of those days, if he had a chance to intervene actively, to respond supportively, or to "resist," and who felt the call to do so, must have come to the conclusion: each action, each supportive response, was too little, too little!

"We did everything wrong!"

"How the suffering came down on all, of which
the earth is filled right to the brim" [a slightly modi-
fied Rilke quotation].

[. . .] It is foremost my sense, my ear for the evidence, [telling me] that you wrote your two volumes
in desperation and that you remain desperate. Moreover, I am convinced: to feel desperation, to remain
desperate, is the dignified and useful attitude we must
adopt when attempting to judge what happened and
to cope with it.

Most of all, I thank you for the understanding
you maintained and gave proof of in the two volumes,
for those who against their wish were pulled into the
vortex of events . . . and who were hence condemned
to do something—and fell short in all their actions.

In this respect, I think mostly of the members of
the Jewish Council, of my Dutch lawyer colleagues,
and last but not least of Dr. [K. J.] Frederiks [Dutch
Secretary General of Internal Affairs], now dead,
whom I greatly appreciated. Certainly he, too, fell
short. He also "did it wrong." But what he wanted and
attempted most fervently, which has sadly been mis-
judged, was pure, filled with good intentions, despite
the fact that I called it wrong-headed as early as 1942.
Dr. Frederiks, indeed, stood in the breach [*Op de bres*
(In the Breach) is the title of Frederiks's book published in The Hague in 1945, in which he defends
his actions during the occupation]. He was braver
than you have recognized. It is true that he helped
only his acquaintances [a reference to the "prominent
Jews" Frederiks protected, sent first to Barneveld and
eventually to Theresienstadt], which even at the time

I deemed basically wrong. In my ignorance I was convinced that one should never do anything for a person in whom one could have a particular interest, or a person one "just liked"! I was afraid that such a motive was bound to have a polluting effect on the acts of helping and saving, at least on their success. However insane this may sound: it seemed to me against God's wish!

Yet a number of young trees in Israel were planted to commemorate some of the acquaintances of Dr. Frederiks [survivors of Theresienstadt], even though they were saved "against God's wish," and [trees were also] planted to commemorate Frederiks himself! Rightly so, I think now! For he is dead. . . . I [also] have to thank you for the careful words you found for my staff member Dr. Wander. Since he is dead and should be counted among those who were killed on the battlefield for a good cause, it is not right to speak of any ambiguity of his purpose or of his part in actions or failures to act. (He was close to the "Red Orchestra," which you and your sources could not have known; his death exempts him from any criticism. Very few of my compatriots risked their lives in active resistance, in "action for Dutch people, for friends," hence for fellow human beings.) . . . In my opinion, your thesis is correct: "All of us were both guilty and innocent at the same time."

Despair is all that is left for the survivors. That this is the case and that this despair is honestly admitted, that is only right and necessary. The writer of *Die Zeit* who reviewed your work asked who would be willing to translate it into German. It is part of my

(I would like to say of "our") despair that we have
to realize: however necessary a translation and publication of such a translation in Germany would be,
it would remain unread. You see, dear Dr. Presser:
nobody listens! Even your compatriots will not trouble themselves with the uncomfortable reading of
your documentation, which is an honest attempt to
do justice to what happened from the perspective of
a historian yet written with fervor. I have friends in
Israel, people I did not help, but who survived. These
friends have urged me for years to let go finally of the
theme that weighs on my heart like a millstone. I am
not able to do that, nor should I. To the prophet Ezekiel, God said: "You must tell them. They will not
harken. Nonetheless you must tell them!"

You have told everything! All the bitterness of
Ezekiel and the other prophets is in your writing, full
of despair.

You should, however, know that here and there a
person, even one whose language is German, is reading
what you wrote. He swallowed the drink that tastes
so bitter to him, a whole tankard full of bitterness
and despair, and he wants to listen. That includes the
obligation to "pass it on." Sadly, on German soil, even
fewer people are willing to listen. (Unfortunately, I
am unable to call my fellow Germans my compatriots.
Ever since 1941, if not since 1933, I consider only the
victims or the dead my compatriots. Only they are
pure, or their death has made them "righteous.")

I know about the despair of those who "survived," of "our common guilt and failure."

There would be so much more to say.

In the end, even about the person whom you
have called frequently by name in your two volumes, quoting him and trying to explain him. The
person you deal with in your two volumes perhaps
too extensively under the name Hans Calmeyer is an
extraordinarily ambiguous fellow. I think that you are
not taking his true measure. He certainly was inad-
equate. You overlooked, as others did, how a sense
of exasperation and bitterness, hence of helplessness,
would dominate a person who as early as 1941, if not
already in 1933, foresaw the "*ondergang*" and who was
aware of the fact that all action and all resistance had
to remain as insufficient as you described it. The words
"too little, too little!" and the question "Is our attempt
to 'save people' according to God's wish?" were written in large letters on each wall C. was facing even
then (which holds true also for the wall on which
others had hung a picture of Hitler!).

What you could not know is that his actions have
never given him "intellectual pleasure," neither then
nor any time up to the present. Already, at the time, he
was as desperate as he is today; he was aware even then
of the wrongness and the inadequacy of all actions and
endeavors. Yet he acted and refrained from acting.
whatever he did or did not do, he did with fervor.

Remaining what I am,
Your Hans Calmeyer[4]

Contrary to Calmeyer's predictions, Presser's two volumes
were best sellers in the Netherlands for decades. But, indeed, this
standard work has not yet been published in German translation.

It was typical for Hans Calmeyer to be the last person he wrote about, and then it was in the third person to preserve distance. I think that his self-criticism was too harsh. All of us who helped, did so within limitations. Besides being Rudi's main support, I also looked after the hidden parents of a Jewish friend and brought them as much sustenance and support as I could. Was that enough, or should I have quit high school to devote myself full time to the underground? Who can pass judgment? I am convinced that Calmeyer did all he could from the vantage point of his office in The Hague. The thousands of lives he saved vouch for that.

Significantly, Calmeyer never mailed that letter to Presser. Purely by chance, it reached its addressee anyway. In 1967, Ben A. Sijes, a staff member of the Dutch Institute for War Documentation (at the time RIOD, now NIOD) visited Calmeyer in order to interview him at the behest of the institute's leader, Dr. Louis de Jong, probably in connection with the upcoming Munich trials. Sijes saw the letter to Jacob Presser on Calmeyer's desk and offered to take it to Presser in Amsterdam.

In the record of the interview, which lasted three and a half hours, Sijes described Calmeyer as a person of culture, well groomed, obliging, but also nervous, depressed, and easily excited. Calmeyer testified, among other things: "There was despair every night. I felt like a murderer."

Sijes observed, "Mr. Calmeyer feels guilty. According to his own pronouncement, he, too, belongs in the dock."[5]

Jacob Presser's favorable appraisal of Calmeyer's years at the Reich Commissariat had not dispelled Calmeyer's self-doubt or his sense of guilt, and it did not relieve the weight on his conscience. Yet, he could not have been indifferent to this acquittal from an eminent Jewish-Dutch historian. Presser, like De Jong, survived the *Shoah*, the former in hiding, the latter in London.

Both lost most of their families, and both made it their preeminent task to research Dutch history from 1940 to 1945, the years of war, occupation, repression, persecution, and annihilation. After the war, the two chroniclers judged Calmeyer's work in The Hague with unequivocal approval.

On July 29, 1967, Presser responded to Calmeyer:

I had the privilege of reading the letter you never mailed to me. You will understand that I prefer a brief reply. I believe that you and I share the essence of our common humanity by recognizing that as survivors of this catastrophe, both of us have to carry a portion of the burden of guilt for the rest of our lives. To which of the two of us is the lighter burden allotted? I for one will never be able to answer: "to me."[6]

Chapter Twenty-five

ACADEME AND REAL LIFE

✤ ✤ ✤

Shortly after I defended my dissertation, I wrote to Otto Frank to ask whether he had any objection to me examining the literary qualities of Anne's *Diary*. He answered in December 1977 that, of course, that would be fine, but he failed to mention that Anne had rewritten her original diary and that two different versions existed. This I learned only in 1986, when the *Critical Edition* of Anne's diaries was published.

Otto's note may well have been the last direct communication I received from him. He died two and a half years later. After his death, Rudi and I visited his widow several times in Basel on our way to or from the Alps.

In the fall of 1978, I was hired by the Portland State University Department of Foreign Languages and Literatures as a full-time, tenure-track faculty member. My record as a successful teacher was known; my research prowess beyond my dissertation still had to be proven. From the beginning, my interest in literature was focused on the context in which a literary work was created, how it related to its era, and what it had to say to its readers and to future generations about that time and place in history. This is what had attracted me to the politically engaged poet and playwright Bertolt Brecht. After focusing on him, I found myself interested in the German documentary theater of the 1960s and published on the subject.

Mother had moved back to the Netherlands in 1975. With my sabbatical drawing near, I looked for a research project that would take me back to Holland. Soon I concentrated on literary works by German refugee artists—Georg Hermann, Grete Weil, Gerhard Durlacher, and, of course, Anne Frank—written after 1933 in the Netherlands, either in German or in Dutch.

Georg Hermann belonged to my grandparents' generation. Born into a nonorthodox Jewish family, he was very progressive, and he was a pacifist. Early in 1933, he fled to the Netherlands, where he published five novels. The last two dealt with the fate of refugees. Before his emigration, Hermann was popular in Germany as the author of the beloved novel *Jettchen Gebert* (*Henriette Gebert*). I published several papers about his works written in the Netherlands and edited a book containing an important late essay and his letters to his daughter in Denmark, written between 1933 and 1941. These letters shed light on the writer's struggle to make a living as a refugee author. Georg Hermann died in 1943, in a train en route to Auschwitz.[1]

The work of Grete Weil, born in 1906, spoke to the aftermath of the experience of the Holocaust in the life of perpetrator, survivor, and victim. For Weil, as for Calmeyer, the war experience was ever present. In the early 1990s, I was privileged to visit Weil—an octogenarian at the time—near Munich. Her husband Edgar had been picked up in the street during the early June 1941 raid in Amsterdam. Edgar had been sent to his death in Mauthausen along with the young agriculture trainees of the Wieringermeer Polder, including our friend Rolf Schwarz. In her work, Weil time and again puts her finger on the wound the

Holocaust inflicted on mankind. Her 1983 semi-autobiograph-
ical novel *Generationen* (Generations) contains the startling
statement: "I suffer from Auschwitz, like others suffer from TB
or cancer. I am as hard to live with as other sufferers."[2]

Gerhard Durlacher and Anne Frank were of my own
generation. Both had been transplanted to the Netherlands as
children of immigrants, and both wrote in Dutch. He survived
several concentration camps, became a lecturer in sociology at
the University of Amsterdam, and wrote five memoirs based on
his experiences as a refugee child and an orphaned Auschwitz
survivor, whose life remained a struggle for fundamental inner
equilibrium. Three of his slim books have been translated into
English and are well worth reading. Anne Frank did not survive.
As a writer, she was robbed of the chance to mature and to learn
from life, but her diary became emblematic of the horrors of a
childhood in wartime under the boot of a hostile occupier. What
most people do not know is the fact that Anne was in the process
of rewriting her diary notes when she and the other seven hiders
were arrested August 4, 1944. Her intention was to publish an
epistolary novel after the war, based on her spontaneous entries
jotted down while in hiding. In my research, I compared her two
versions and was struck by her quick growth as a writer.

After I secured a small research stipend from the Dutch
government, Rudi and I settled for most of 1985 in the historic
town of Leiden, Rembrandt's birthplace. There I could work at
the Netherlands' oldest university, while Rudi joined a research
group in nearby Delft at the Technical Institute, where he had
first registered as a student in 1946.

One circle had closed. Our wartime experiences were receding into history, and new pressing issues demanded our attention. In the early 1980s, students had asked Rudi what he had to say about the nuclear energy plant downriver from Portland. To his embarrassment, Rudi had to confess that he had not given it much thought. He promised to study the matter, and that led him to become an activist.

After thirty years of basic nuclear research, Rudi ventured down from the ivory tower of academe into the turmoil surrounding the health hazards of ionizing radiation. He told the story to Elke Stenzel for her 2009 book *Den Nazis eine schallende Ohrfeige versetzen* (Giving the Nazis a resounding slap in the face):

> I started reading the pertinent scientific literature, [. . .] and the more I delved into this whole issue, the more I realized how dishonestly the research findings had been interpreted by official radiation health scientists. They had allowed themselves to be influenced and corrupted by money, power, and career considerations. As I became aware of the radioactive contamination around the Hanford nuclear site, I joined Oregon Physicians for Social Responsibility (PSR), an affiliate of the Nobel Prize–winning organization International Physicians for the Prevention of Nuclear War (IPPNW).
>
> Hanford is located in our neighbor state of Washington. The plutonium produced there was used for the bomb on Nagasaki and, subsequently, for thousands and thousands more atomic weapons. And, of course, Hanford workers and the population around Hanford were affected. Yet, the government had always claimed there were no detrimental health effects.

I got to know a number of astute women who residing downwind from Hanford (Downwinders). Coordinating their efforts in a quest for meaningful answers [...] these women had been routinely brushed off by the government and by the official authorities as "emotional housewives."

I started an extensive research project on the health effects among Hanford Downwinders. We developed and evaluated more than eight hundred questionnaires on human health with minimal financial support and with volunteers [Downwinders and members of PSR] doing all the work. Laureen was very much part of this project; she helped plan it and she critiqued it, and it was she who organized the work of the volunteers, which took hundreds of person hours of transcribing the data and evaluating them.[3]

Fortunately, we had the invaluable help of a PSR physician friend, Charles M. Grossman, MD, for medical evaluations, and the aid of our son Fred, who designed a database for computerized analysis. After five years of intensive work, Rudi succeeded in getting our findings published in refereed journals.[4]

Rudi's commitment to the victims of nuclear radiation was closely connected to his experiences of going into hiding during the war. He continued in Stenzel's book:

On the one hand, I was reminded of the lies and propaganda of the Nazis, which so many people had believed, and of the concomitant insight that people are easily seduced by any kind of ideology. On the other hand, there was the memory of very simple people who had put their life on the line when I had to go into hiding.

The people around Hanford had been deceived
and lied to in the name of patriotism. In a free
democracy, they had been prevented from adequately
protecting their health and that of their children. I
felt called upon to help them with my knowledge and
prestige as an independent scientist.[5]

Time and again, the activist group of women around Hanford
wrote to tell Rudi how important it was for them that a scientist and
a physician had taken them seriously, instead of telling them they
were suffering from "radiophobia" and had better see a psychiatrist.

One woman quoted Rudi as saying, "You Downwinders are
suffering from betrayal, and believe me, I know all about betrayal."

She continued, "Dr. Nussbaum drew parallels between
Nazi atrocities and the experiences of Hanford Downwinders.
The experimentation at Hanford on thousands of unsuspecting
humans with lethal doses of radiation shares some aspects of
inhumanity with the barbaric experimentation and slaughter
at Auschwitz and Dachau . . . [yet] because they didn't target
their experiments on a particular race or religion . . . it cannot
be called genocide."[6]

Chapter Twenty-six

WRESTLING THE PAST

✣ ✣ ✣

In the late 1940s, Calmeyer had avidly followed the Nuremberg Trials. They had been held by an international military tribunal followed by a series of American, British, and French military tribunals. After statehood in 1949, the Federal Republic of Germany (FRG) was responsible for prosecuting former Nazis in the western part of the country, and in the eastern part, the courts of the German Democratic Republic (GDR) were given similar responsibility by the Soviet Union. FRG court cases against the former Nazis suffered from the problem that many Nazi crimes went beyond the scope of codified criminal law, which did not include the possibility of a criminal state. In murder cases, the law distinguished between the perpetrator, who did the deed "of his own free will," and the accomplice, who merely assisted him.

From its beginning, the legal system of the Federal Republic was prepared to categorize only the top commanders as the real National Socialist (NS) perpetrators—Hitler, Himmler, Heydrich, Göring, Goebbels, Bormann—and to accuse all others as guilty "only" of aiding and abetting. The net result was that the cadre of the *Reichsbahn*, the German railroad system, on which the annihilation camps depended, as well as that of the *Reichssicherheitshauptamt* (RSHA), the main office of Reich Security, with its hundreds of "desk criminals," were not criminally prosecuted.

The number of Nazi trials increased after the 1958 trial in Ulm of members of the Nazi *Einsatzgruppen* (hit squads). A central office was set up to coordinate law enforcement pertaining to crimes of violence during the war in the different states. In the early 1960s, the central office acquired the records of the RSHA from the United States, containing the names of eight thousand perpetrators (with their ranks) and 2,700 witnesses, as well as 150,000 dossiers. No major trials ensued, since the West German justice administration sentenced only "excessive perpetrators" for murder. All others were considered "accomplices" and released, if they were tried at all.

The second problem was the statute of limitations. Prosecutions for lesser offenses (including "deprivation of freedom") were barred by the statute of limitations as early as May 9, 1955, ten years after the end of the war. As the end of the statutory period of limitations approached, the problem was discussed in the *Bundestag*. The statutory period of limitations was not extended, although anyone could see that many perpetrators would go unpunished unless a large number of crimes were investigated and clarified. After May 9, 1960, all crimes punishable with fifteen years behind bars were no longer a chargeable offense after fifteen years from the date the offense was committed. Included were physical injury and "deprivation of freedom *with lethal consequences.*"

In the rewritten §50 (2) of the *Strafgesetzbuch* (criminal code), the punishment to be meted out for those who aided and abetted manslaughter without base motives was pushed into the fifteen-year category. Hence, all the "desk perpetrators" who knew about the base motives of their superiors without sharing them would no longer be prosecuted. From then on, no perpetrators were left between the highest leaders, who had issued the orders, and the lowly actual murderers of the concentration and annihilation camps.

This failure to do justice apparently went unnoticed in the West German judiciary system. Nor did the *Bundesgerichtshof* (BGH), the highest federal court, or the attorneys working as public prosecutors for that court, raise objections. The German Socialist Party (SPD), which Calmeyer supported, presented two bills seeking to extend the statute of limitations, but both were turned down.[1]

The political climate in Germany finally began to change in the late 1960s. In October 1969, Willy Brandt, a Social Democrat and anti-Nazi who had spent the Hitler years in exile in Sweden, became chancellor of the FRG. It was a period of radical protests, marches, and demonstrations not just in Germany, but all across the West. Students in Berlin chanted, "Paint the blue flower red!" calling for the fusty older generation of restoration to give way to a society that was fair and equitable. This rambunctious young generation of West Germans supported Brandt and challenged their elders' self-serving excuses for the Nazis still in high positions.

Calmeyer welcomed the overdue developments, but he had lost faith in the possibility of a different Germany. A client quoted him as saying, half-heartedly, "Perhaps things will now change for the better."[2]

Gradually, Hans Calmeyer was withdrawing from the world. He had enjoyed writing occasional poems since his university years. The poetry he committed to paper in the 1960s had a bleak tone:

You know it was the darkness
we had to live through. Our time
was gloom weighed down by guilt.
It is alive still. Of this I am sure:
Guilt darkens, it remains quite real.
Where could we fit in lightness here?
. . .
Why am I hesitating in the dark?
A burdened conscience? Try to understand:
Light's blinding me. It makes me blink.
Look, here I come. There is a song inside me
composed of light. I realize:
What counts is to be blithe.[3]

Calmeyer must have been responding to expressions of irritation provoked by his incessant gloomy comments. Those in his innermost circle were tired of hearing about his dissatisfaction with developments in the FRG, the political and judicial glossing over of Nazi crimes, the "millstone" of personal guilt he carried with him. In the twenty years following the war, he reproached himself more and more for having done "too little" to help the Jews of the Netherlands.

Finally, in the mid-1960s, there were signs of a revitalization of "Lucky Hans" Calmeyer. The Dutch Institute for War Documentation holds a fifteen-page draft of a letter Calmeyer wrote to Günter Prey, a colleague and friend in The Hague during the Nazi years. Written in March 1966, the typescript has many handwritten additions he must have deemed too private even for the eyes of his secretaries. It is a moving testimony to Calmeyer's expectations of the court case being prepared in Munich against the "desk criminals" of the occupation government in the Netherlands.

Calmeyer anticipated to be called to Munich as a witness in the trials of three important defendants. The first was the former head of the SD, later SS brigade commander, Dr. Wilhelm Harster. Following his deployment in the Netherlands, Harster became an SS squad commander in Italy; after the war, he made a career as higher government counsellor in the State of Bavaria. Also to be tried were Assault Company Commander Wilhelm Zoepf, Calmeyer's longtime adversary, who had worked directly under Adolf Eichmann, and Zoepf's overzealous secretary Gertrud Slottke.

Calmeyer's letter to Prey must have served as mental preparation for Munich. He wrote: "For a long time, I have been convinced that the individual crimes of the genocide have to be brought before a German court for their trial. Our compatriots are the murderers; compatriots must pass sentence upon them."

Harster, he pointed out, was a lawyer who rose through the police ranks. He thought it important to know how and why Harster came to join the SS in order to determine how much he stood behind the genocide orders.

About Zoepf's guilt, he had no question. Zoepf, too, was a lawyer, and he was a man of superior intelligence and artistic sensibility. Calmeyer was sure he had voluntarily embraced the SS philosophy. For Calmeyer, Zoepf stood as a prime example of the many Nazi-era lawyers who suffered from a kind of schizophrenia:

> "In uniform"—that is to say, as long as a person functioned as a member of one of the Nazi institutions—he or she knew only too well about the murdering. That was an integral part of the profession of a "political soldier." Just as a nation, a people, and a state were beyond and above the moral order, a person in uniform was

allowed everything and could not be prosecuted. The moment he donned his uniform, he was free of any responsibility. He stood outside the moral order, was allowed to act without benefit of his conscience, and could not be sued. . . . I have asked countless contemporaries, mainly lawyers, who answered me quite seriously: . . . The nation is allowed everything in its struggle for existence. Only the individual can be held responsible, not the hands the nation needs in its struggle for life. . . . Coming back to Zoepf: . . . The one side of this schizophrenia was the very artistically inclined Wilhelm Zoepf; the other side was the same Zoepf in uniform: a cold-blooded murderer who sent 93,000 or more people to their death with no pangs of conscience. . . . The higher the intelligence of the perpetrator, the guiltier he is.[4]

Calmeyer had little to say about the infamous Gertrud Slottke, whose merciless rejections of pleas for deferment were notorious in Camp Westerbork. Calmeyer did not know her as well as the two other defendants. Her background needed to be thoroughly checked, he wrote. Since she came from the Danzig area, she may have been from a Polish-speaking family. What was she doing when the German troops marched into Poland? Under what circumstances did she join the SS? Like Harster and Zoepf, she must have known what happened to the Jews once the trains carried them across the Dutch border to the East.

Calmeyer looked forward to testifying at the Munich trials. Precisely because of his close involvement with the Reich Commissariat at The Hague in 1941–1945, he believed he could make valuable contributions in court. He also sensed that the experience would be personally cathartic. But it was not to be.

The three defendants, unlike most of the other Nazis prosecuted after the war, pled guilty.[5]

German-born American lawyer Robert M. W. Kempner, who had fled the Nazis via Italy to the United States, returned to Germany after the end of World War II to help prosecute Nazi war criminals at Nuremberg. Kempner was an eloquent assistant prosecutor in the Munich trial as well, where he represented two of the millions killed by the Nazis: Carmelite nun Edith Stein, and young Jewish diarist Anne Frank. By singling out these two well-known Holocaust victims, both deported from the Netherlands, Kempner gave focus to the unimaginable. He published his contributions to the trial in the augmented second edition of his book *SS im Kreuzverhör* [SS under cross-examination], released in 1987.[6]

The fact that a German criminal court tried and convicted the white-collar criminals of The Hague must have met Calmeyer's approval and likely helped to relieve his burdened conscience. The trial took place over twenty years after the crimes were committed, but a heavy guilt had been addressed, and the individuals responsible were finally punished.

Calmeyer developed an interest in the religious philosophy of Herman Weidelener, an Augsburg pastor who fused the Christianity of St. John the Evangelist with Taoist and Zen Buddhist teachings. In a letter to his aunt, Calmeyer explained that the practice of meditation was like swimming in the breakers:

> The most important thing is that one dispenses with thinking. One should be nothing to oneself, not even a feather, only a part of the wave. One has to abandon oneself to the wave. Then you fly, you simply fly, you are a part of the sea, a part of everything, until the wave deposits you gently on the beach. . . . Only the

person who is light as a feather will ride it out—in
the surf as well as in life. You experience the moment
when you are nothing, nothing at all.[7]

Was it morose that Calmeyer liked to visit cemeteries and study
inscriptions on the gravestones?[8] With this predeliction for epi-
taphs, it is not surprising that he composed an epitaph for himself:

He wanted a great deal, craved a great deal,
burnt up and decaying, he still did not feel
he had met a single goal for real.[9]

Chapter Twenty-seven

PREPARING FOR DEATH

✢ ✢ ✢

In the summer of 1971, at the age of sixty-eight, Calmeyer suffered a mild heart attack. In response, he wrote his last will and testament:

Before I set out—by myself—on the long road,
and hence in any case:

I want to be cremated.
The announcement may read:
Hans Georg C.
June 23, 1903–July 10, 1971
He called himself "Lucky Hans."

He said:
We do not know God's ways;
we do not even know the way to him.
But we know the upward direction of the arrow.

He wrote:
I wanted a great deal, craved a great deal,
burnt up and decaying, I still did not feel
I'd met a single goal for real.

But no harm is done, if the emotion
guiding my life reached you—just a spark
short-lived like a candle before it gets dark,
the sound still audible that caused a commotion
struggling within me for so long
to unfold in a song.

Do not forget to add Michael's name under the announcement.

I believe "I am well on my way!"
I am at peace, in this respect too,
I have always been a Lucky Hans.
July 7, 1971 C[1]

*Hans Calmeyer in 1972, just weeks
before his death*

When he composed his final testament, Hans Calmeyer believed himself closer to the end of his life than he really was. In June of 1972, his son Peter, who had become a professor of archaeology and a renowned Iranologist, married a colleague, Ursula Seidl, a distinguished archaeologist in her own right. For the wedding, Calmeyer traveled to Berlin alone; Ruth was again ailing. Ursula Seidl-Calmeyer noticed to her surprise that her new father-in-law was carrying unopened letters from the United States in his coat pocket. They were from his second son, Michael. Ursula surmised that Calmeyer feared they might contain reproaches against him.[2] More likely, though, these letters pertained to Michael's plans to visit his father later that summer.

Since Ines and ten-year-old Michael had left for the United States in 1963, Hans Calmeyer had met his second son only once, very briefly, in 1970. Forty-five years later, Michael remembered the encounter:

> I was 17 and [our meeting was] for less than 30 minutes. He came out to Schiphol Airport in the Netherlands during the summer as I was traveling on a Euro Pass with a friend and it just never happened that the travel schedule with my friend was able to accommodate a visit to Osnabrück. As it was, there was a discomfort in even the idea of impinging on Ruth .... But it was there at the airport that we had a first mature conversation ... quite amazing and odd for me as a young and relatively inexperienced traveler to suddenly meet my dad at the airport. I wished I could have spent a lot more time with him that summer .... I feel even today a deep pang of regret that that was such a short meeting. I tried to make up for that in the next trip ... and a visit was

planned for the next time, which could not happen for another 2 years.

The second visit was when he died on the same night I got there. I was moped'ing through Europe on a 35 mph Mobylette I had bought in Paris and riding 6,000 km all over Europe including England, Spain and Italy etc. And so, I stopped by with a little more preparation to stay at my dad's, to also meet his wife seemingly for the first time though we had met at some length sometime . . . before my mother and I left Germany at age 10.

I got in with my little moped and was told that my father had just had a heart attack . . . and that he was so glad to see me after recuperating for a week. We took for granted that he would recover, but he was weak. . . . I got in [after dinner] in the evening and for some reason I don't recall seeing the wife at that time but perhaps she was already going to sleep. . . . [M]y father and I proceeded to spend three hours together just talking in his living room. The conversation was totally comfortable . . . never forced or strange, always loving and gentle. . . . Nothing really about his history was ever mentioned. I would only learn his life story a little bit from my mother after he died, and then much more deeply from Peter Niebaum many years later.

My father did say the following parting words to me at the end of that last evening, which I did not quite appreciate until the next morning: "I am now finally happy and complete in my life." . . . [T]here was the clear sense that he had been waiting for me to get there in the week after his heart attack.

That night between September 2 and 3, 1972, Hans Calmeyer died from heart failure. Michael described the room in which his father died:

> He was in a bedroom as sparse as a jail cell, with a cot for a bed and a simple nightstand as the only furniture. I believe it was recreating his cell in Holland, or something terribly ascetic from the prison camps that only monks tend to do. He was not depressed per se toward the end, but very conscious of his desire to have saved all of the people he encountered in Holland.

Michael closed his father's eyes and brought down his arms, which had been uplifted.

In an email dated July 11, 2015, he wrote: "I went over to the wife and we hugged for a long time. I was conscious of the blessing of being there to comfort her; that is about the only real reaction I could have." He waited with Ruth for Peter to arrive from his archaeological dig in Iran. Michael's civilized but cool relations with his father's wife became almost loving as they mourned together for a week and a real bond developed. During the subsequent year, Ruth and Michael exchanged meaningful letters until Michael let the correspondence lapse.

As to his own mother, Michael Calmeyer Hentschel wrote that Ines died in his arms in January 2014 from a combination of dementia and a number of strokes that left her quite disabled. "She was a simple, loving person who did not seek complications. . . . She dearly loved Hans Calmeyer her whole life, and I did not question any of it, understanding the depth of her love and respect for him only after slowly learning his background not from her but from Peter Niebaum."

Most of the wishes Hans Calmeyer expressed in his last will and testament of July 7, 1971, were not fulfilled. There was no private obituary notice, only the official announcement by the Bar Association, which bore no mention of Michael. Calmeyer was not cremated, perhaps because in 1972 urns were not interred in traditional burials. Funeral services took place in the facilities of Osnabrück's Heger Cemetery, which easily accommodated the modest number of participants. Hans-Heinrich Gurland, a protestant minister and brother of Rolf Gurland, Calmeyer's partner in the law firm, led the memorial services. In correspondence, Calmeyer had asked the clergyman to call him neither a hero nor a Christian, a wish that was presumably honored.

Calmeyer's friend since early childhood, fellow lawyer Eberhard Westerkamp, spoke briefly at the memorial:

> Our friend Hans Calmeyer's intelligent mind and warm heart—always quietly wide open for his fellow beings, whether close by or far away—were early on filled with the decisive strength of a wise person, ready to extend himself in any circumstance. In the unchanged personality of Hans [after World War II], his acquaintances, including those who felt real friendship for him, . . . recognized the familiar eccentric. He still seemed to go his own special ways—or not to go them—in any case, went about life somehow differently from how they themselves did. Unnoticeable to everyone except his wife, the black events of the past accompanied him, as if they had become his own shadow. In the end, nothing mattered to him anymore but that which could bring a glimmer of light into the gloom.[3]

Ruth Calmeyer lived to be an octogenarian despite her perennial medical problems. She died on February 6, 1988. Her last address was Friedrichstrasse 48, the Calmeyer family residence, where she and Hans had moved with baby Peter fifty-seven years before.

Claus Cronemeyer, a young Osnabrück physician who looked after Ruth for the last nine years of her life, remembers his frequent home visits rather fondly. Her kidney and bladder ailments had subsided, and her health was robust. Dr. Cronemeyer felt he was called less to administer to her physical needs than for her spiritual well-being.

During their visits, Ruth's mind was on the past. She told Dr. Cronemeyer about her husband's courageous activities during World War II. The good doctor eventually passed her story on to his friend Peter Niebaum, who began to delve into it immediately after Ruth Calmeyer's death.[4]

Chapter Twenty-eight

A Circle Closes

❖ ❖ ❖

Quite unexpectedly Hans Calmeyer came back into my life when, in 1988, Rudi was invited to speak about his research into the health effects of low-level radiation at a conference in Münster, Germany. In nearby Osnabrück he met with the local IPPNW group (International Physicians for the Prevention of Nuclear War). His hosts were a young pediatrician and his wife, Klaus and Eva Muck. They showed great interest in our survival story, and we developed a close friendship with them. Their daughter Nina was the same age as our oldest granddaughter, Robin. When the two girls were juniors in high school, we arranged for a three months' exchange during the school year 1993–1994. One of Nina's teachers, Peter Niebaum, was working on a biography of Hans Calmeyer.

I remembered, of course, the all-important Calmeyer list during the war years, and I had read what Presser wrote about that extraordinary German lawyer in *Ondergang* (*Ashes in the Wind*). I also recalled how for years, on Saint Nicholas eve, my parents sent a small remembrance to Mr. Kotting, our lawyer, who had succeeded in getting my mother "Aryanized," and in doing so had saved our family from the death camps. None of us, however, had looked beyond Mr. Kotting to the official at the Reich Commissariat who had made the crucial decision.

In 1992, prompted by Peter Niebaum, the Israeli Holocaust Memorial Museum, Yad Vashem, bestowed upon Hans Calmeyer the title "Righteous Among the Nations." A tree was planted in his name. Following the suggestions of Niebaum's Calmeyer Initiative, the city of Osnabrück named a square and a school for its honored citizen, Hans Calmeyer. In 1995, in a ceremony attended by the Israeli ambassador Avi Primor, the city posthumously awarded its highest distinction, the Möser medal, to Calmeyer. His son Peter, by then professor emeritus of archaeology, received it in his father's name.[1]

Rudi and I were most eager to meet Peter Niebaum. He told us how in the late 1980s he had heard Calmeyer's story from his friend, Dr. Claus Cronemeyer, Ruth Calmeyer's physician. Ever since, he had devoted his life to finding out more about the brave and resourceful anti-Nazi lawyer, a fellow native of Osnabrück. Despite daunting setbacks, Niebaum wrote a biography of great length but could not find a publisher. The city of Osnabrück's support, which had allowed him a reduced teaching load while he researched and wrote, ran out when the city fathers became leery of the project. They had consulted the Dutch Institute for War Documentation (NIOD) to substantiate Niebaum's assertions about Hans Calmeyer's role in saving thousands of Jewish lives, but the NIOD was less than supportive. Calmeyer still was a controversial figure in the Netherlands.

Nonetheless, the local Calmeyer Initiative, banking on Peter Niebaum's research, invited NIOD historian Coenraad Stuldreher to come and speak. I happened to be in Germany, and on November 11, 1998, I took a quick side trip to listen to Stuldreher's talk in Osnabrück's historic city hall.

Stuldreher's presentation upset me terribly. It was a truly disgraceful performance. The speaker said that he had looked through a large sample of files and had not found a single forged document on the strength of which Calmeyer had made a positive decision. He concluded that there was no reason to assume Hans Calmeyer had actively tried to save Jewish lives. Afterward, I went up to remonstrate with him on the basis of my own mother's case. He was not familiar with it, nor did he care to learn more. That night, I jotted down, "Peter Niebaum was fuming." This was not the last stab in his back by "experts" from the NIOD.

After the sensational negative evaluation by Coenraad Stuldreher, Osnabrück city officials were no longer sure that Hans Calmeyer *was* a hero. They asked the NIOD for an expert report, which was duly put together by yet another Dutch historian, Dr. Geraldien von Frijtag Drabbe-Künzel, and presented in the year 2000. According to her research, Calmeyer had undoubtedly accepted petitions based on forged materials. All the same, nothing proved that clever Dutch lawyers had not duped him. If in fact Calmeyer had been aware of what was going on and attempted to help the persecuted Jews, why did he not decide in favor of more Jewish petitioners?

Dr. Von Frijtag Drabbe-Künzel concluded that Calmeyer was part and parcel of the occupiers' killing machine. Calmeyer's actions, she found, had been self-serving—saving some hundreds of Jews may have been a mere by-product of his assignment at the Reich Commissariat, a job that spared him from being sent to the front lines.[2]

Peter Niebaum kept us well informed about the controversies swirling around his Calmeyer biography. He had put his all into that book; not only the results of his careful research into Calmeyer's life, but also his own observations and misgivings about German politics between the two World Wars and after the defeat of 1945. Finally, in the summer of 2001, three circumspect editors saw Peter Niebaum's *Ein Gerechter unter den Völkern. Hans Calmeyer in seiner Zeit (1903–1972)* [A Righteous Man Among the Nations. Hans Calmeyer in his time (1903–1972)] through the publication process. I was asked to write a foreword. Here was my chance to thank the man who had saved my family's lives. I welcomed Niebaum's book as a rectification of the neglect and misunderstanding Calmeyer had suffered.

The fall of 2001 found Rudi and me back in Osnabrück. We were delighted when Peter Niebaum handed us a copy of his Calmeyer book with an appreciative dedication. Hans Calmeyer's story needed to be accessible in English, so I urged Peter Niebaum to write a shorter version of his book, which I would translate for readers in the United States and elsewhere. He said he would think over my suggestion. We corresponded about it for a while until I dropped the subject. My attention to the Calmeyer project had been painfully diverted.

In July of 2003, our daughter was diagnosed with stage 4 breast cancer. For the next several years, I did very little research but instead focused on Elka and her family. Between the doctors' visits and the chemotherapy sessions there were good weeks, even months. For a pleasant break, Rudi and I took Elka with us to the Oregon Shakespeare Festival in Ashland, and, along with her husband, on our sailing trips in the Puget Sound. Here we could forget the disease and stress, calmed by the water, mountains, islands, and wildlife.

In February 2007, we had a heartwarming living memorial for Elka. She passed away on Good Friday, April 6, 2007, barely fifty years old.

Chapter Twenty-nine

A DEVASTATING LOSS

✤ ✤ ✤

It was hard to continue life without Elka. Rudi and I returned to our weekly volunteer work at the Oregon Food Bank, where we had joined a team in the fall of 2001. After all, we had known hunger! We were also active as speakers of the Oregon Holocaust Resource Center, which was created after the first Anne Frank exhibition came to Portland in 1992. Like the other members of the Resource Center's Speakers Bureau, we talked about our experiences during World War II in middle schools and high schools all over Oregon and southwest Washington. We also presented to adult audiences in libraries and other venues.

When the second Anne Frank exhibit was shown in Portland in 2002, Rudi and I were scheduled to speak to classes every Monday morning at Portland's oldest shopping center. I always focused on Anne's great gift as a writer and on her literary development, pointing out how her admirable growth as an author could be traced from her original diary entries to her thorough revision less than two years later.

Both Rudi and I emphasized what made the Holocaust possible during the Nazi era and delineated the disconcerting

Rudi and Laureen in the Portland Rose Garden, 2008

parallels we saw in our world at the beginning of the new mil-
lennium. Democracy was falling apart here in the USA, just the
way it had in Germany in the interbellum years. Exceptionalism
and expansionism were accepted as basic to a patriotic stance.
We encouraged our listeners to think critically and to look at the
roles they were playing in their own society and beyond. Then
a docent would take the audience to the beginning of the panel
section of the exhibit. In a letter to us she confirmed how urgent
it was to bear witness.

Dear Professors,

On Monday mornings the students come to the panel
section soon after they hear you speak. I'm the first
docent in the panel section, so sometimes they come
straight from you to me. I ask them to tell me about
you. They always tell me that they have never heard
a life story like yours before. Even the most reluctant

students tell me this when I ask, and I always want to thank you, at this point, for being here, for professing, for telling people over and over. I think you are the most important contact that all these students have made here.

Thank you,
Mary Collier
April 29, 2002[1]

When we visited the Mucks, our Osnabrück friends, in May of 2009, we talked with Peter Niebaum over a cup of tea in his wife's exquisite garden. We learned that upon Niebaum's suggestion a young neighbor of his, Mathias Middelberg, had written his doctoral dissertation in the field of law about Hans Calmeyer's legal and extra-legal activities in the Netherlands. Middelberg's *Judenrecht, Judenpolitik und der Jurist Hans Calmeyer in den besetzten Niederlanden, 1940–1945* (Jew laws, Jew politics and the jurist Hans Calmeyer in the occupied Netherlands, 1940–1945) had appeared in 2005.

The study fully corroborated Niebaum's findings of 2001. Moreover, even as we spoke, a Dutch lawyer, Ruth van Galen-Herrmann, was writing a rebuttal to Dr. Geraldien von Frijtag Drabbe-Künzel's "expert" report of the year 2000 and to that historian's subsequent book *Het geval Calmeyer* (the Calmeyer case), published in Amsterdam in 2008. This was exciting news, and it was good to see Peter Niebaum encouraged. I reiterated the idea of a short Calmeyer biography as a template for an English translation, and Peter Niebaum was amenable to the suggestion. He soon went to work.

Later that year, Ruth van Galen-Herrmann's book appeared: *Calmeyer, dader of mensenredder? Visies op Calmeyers rol in de jodenvervolging* (Calmeyer, perpetrator or rescuer? Views of Calmeyer's role in the persecution of the Jews). Van Galen-Herrmann found no fault with Von Frijtag Drabbe-Künzel's research, but she took issue with the historian's interpretation of Calmeyer's motives.

The mistaken analysis was based, Van Galen-Herrmann wrote, on the theories of Ulrich Herbert, a contemporary German sociologist who had studied the members of his country's Nazi leadership elite born between 1900 and 1909. They had come of age right after the defeat of 1919. Hans Calmeyer's adversaries Erich Rajakowitsch and Wilhelm Zoepf belonged to that age group, as did Adolf Eichmann. Many of Herbert's sociological insights apply to these men.

Since Calmeyer, born in 1903, was part of the same cohort, and as a lawyer belonged to the elite, Von Frijtag Drabbe-Künzel argued that he must have been motivated by the same revanchist and anti-Semitic convictions as the majority of his contemporaries.[2] Calmeyer's use of Nazi jargon in memos concerning the Jews of the Netherlands was seen as proof of his base convictions even though he was never a member of the Nazi Party. Von Frijtag Drabbe-Künzel had made no allowance for possible subterfuge on Calmeyer's part, and she attributed his decisions in favor of Jewish petitioners to a craving for recognition rather than to the wish to save Jewish lives. Calmeyer was part of a criminal system, she reasoned, therefore a perpetrator. If he had really opposed the persecution of the Jews, he should have resigned from his post.[3]

Van Galen-Herrmann refuted these negative judgments one by one. In her closing remarks, she called for more research into the dossiers of petitioners, mainly because the number of Jews Calmeyer saved from deportation had been approximated as 3,700, while the actual number was probably much higher.[4]

Van Galen-Herrmann saw Hans Calmeyer unequivocally

as a rescuer, not a perpetrator. Her conclusions heartened Peter Niebaum as he set about to write a short Calmeyer biography. He promised it would be ready by the summer of 2011, and he kept his word.

In mid-June of 2011, Rudi and I flew to Europe for what we thought would be our last Swiss hiking trip. We retraced some of the hikes we had taken in 1950, during our (belated) honeymoon. From Switzerland, we took the train to Osnabrück to attend the launching of Peter Niebaum's short biography, *Hans Calmeyer—ein "anderer Deutscher" im 20. Jahrhundert* (Hans Calmeyer—a "different German" of the 20th century). The ceremony took place in the city hall, where the Peace of Westphalia had been signed in 1648, at the end of the Thirty Years' War that had laid the country to waste. The portraits of the seventeenth-century signatories looked down on us from the walls of the room.

The mayor opened the gathering called by the Calmeyer Initiative. Since Niebaum's new biography was published by the same publishing house as Elke Stenzel's *Den Nazis eine schallende Ohrfeige versetzen*, Stenzel was on hand to read from her compilation of resistance stories. Then Peter Niebaum commented on reflections in the afterword to his new book. As we parted, I promised him that I would get to work on the translation of *Ein anderer Deutscher* upon our return to Portland.

That was not to be. On our way home, we stopped for a few days in Amsterdam to see family and friends. The day of our departure, July 20, 2011, Rudi and I were searching Schiphol airport for a place to buy salted raw herring, our favorite Dutch treat. Rudi, pushing our carry-on bags in a small luggage cart, did not notice a set of steps, fell down, and broke his neck. He split his second cervical vertebra and could not breathe or move his limbs. Passersby applied CPR.

Once on oxygen, Rudi regained consciousness. He could hear, yet he could only respond by raising his eyebrows. I found it hard to accept that he could not even squeeze my hand. Dutch physicians in a nearby hospital kept him artificially alive until our sons and their wives could fly over to bid him farewell. Fortunately, my Dutch family, a nephew and his wife as well as my two nieces, were right there, and they were wonderfully supportive.

Two days later, Rudi's and my life together ended in Amsterdam where it had begun seventy years earlier. Another circle had closed. I tried to remind myself that Rudi had worried about infirmity, a gradual loss of his capacity to lead a full life. He was eighty-nine years old and we had enjoyed a wonderful hiking vacation in the Alps. I persuaded myself to be grateful that he was spared decline and that his life had ended quickly, on a high note. A dozen Dutch and German friends joined the family at the cremation. Son Fred played his cello, as he had done at his father's bedside. Ralph, our oldest, led the ceremony.

Back home in Portland, we had a deeply moving memorial for Rudi, attended by some three hundred people: friends, colleagues, Downwinders, physicians from PSR, neighbors, teammates from the Food Bank, fellow speakers from the Holocaust Resource Center. That was a great comfort to me and to our family.

Chapter Thirty

FULFILLING MY PROMISE

✢ ✢ ✢

I decided to sell our condo and move to Seattle, where Ralph and Carol had made their home for well over thirty years. My children helped me with the packing and unpacking and with a great deal of paperwork. Still, it took until the end of 2012 before I was completely settled at University House, a most stimulating retirement community. Only then did I begin the translation of Niebaum's Calmeyer biography.

It soon became clear to me that whole sections of the book were geared toward German readers. The chapters about Calmeyer's childhood, his education, and his life after the end of World War II would require many footnotes to make the text intelligible to English-language readers. It would be better to rewrite the book with an international public in mind. Fortunately, a former Portland State colleague linked me up with a seasoned co-author, Karen Kirtley, who insisted that I add my own history to that of Hans Calmeyer and show how the two were interrelated. Alas, I could not seek Peter Niebaum's approval. He died from cancer in September 2013 at age seventy.

Like most survivors, I am prone to unexpected flashbacks.
While I was working on this book, I repeatedly had a curious
experience. In University House, residents are urged to wear
their magnetic name tags whenever they leave their apartment
so newcomers have an easier time learning names. While writing,
I lived intensely in the past, and so, when I wanted to go down
for dinner, I told myself more than once, "Don't forget to put on
your star . . . uh, name tag!"

*Mathias Middelberg's book cover. Behind
the picture of Calmeyer is a copy of the
Kleins' Aryanization document!*

Early in 2015, news from Europe reached me that Mathias
Middelberg was rewriting and updating his doctoral dissertation. In April of that year, he published his very readable *"Wer
bin ich, dass ich über Leben und Tod entscheide?" Hans Calmeyer*

"Rassenreferent" in den Niederlanden 1941-1945 ["Who am I that I should decide about life and death?" Hans Calmeyer, in charge of race-related decisions in the Netherlands, 1941-1945]. He kindly sent a copy of his new book just in time for me to incorporate some of his recent findings into this text.

Cognizant of the fact that Hans Calmeyer is still a controversial figure in some quarters, Middelberg titled his last chapter *"Schindler oder Schwindler—das Fazit"* ("Schindler or Swindler—the Upshot"). He concluded that Calmeyer decided at least 3,709 cases in favor of petitioners and their family members. In addition, the protracted period of time their cases were "pending" in Calmeyer's office gave a sizable number of Jews the opportunity to find a place to hide. Moreover, Calmeyer's principled stance on exempting the nine thousand Jewish partners in mixed marriages from deportation, a stance that was eventually adopted by the Reich Commissar, arguably added to the number of those whose lives he helped spare.

When Calmeyer claimed in his defense of 1946 that he had saved seventeen thousand Jewish lives, he must have counted all the categories mentioned, plus the close to one thousand Portuguese Jews he assumed had survived in *Theresienstadt* (Terezin). Sadly, they had not. Yet, all in all, Calmeyer saved many more Jewish lives than his famous compatriot Oskar Schindler, credited with saving up to 1,200.[1]

Benno Stokvis, one of the Amsterdam lawyers who frequently brought cases to Calmeyer's office, remembered his experiences in a commemorative article, "Deceit in Grand Style in Order to Save Human Life." Stokvis summarized, "For a person who was 'Aryanized,' the gate to life opened."[2]

Hans Calmeyer's daughter-in-law, Ursula Seidl-Calmeyer, called my attention to a Dutch study about the fate of the Portuguese Jews in the Netherlands during the German occupation,

Jaap Cohen, *De onontkoombare afkomst van Eli d'Oliveira. Een Portugees-Joodse familiegeschiedenis* [The inescapable ancestry of Eli d'Oliveira. A Portuguese-Jewish family history], published in Amsterdam in 2015.

In this hefty tome Hans Calmeyer is mentioned thirty times, frequently in extended passages. He is shown to be the one German official who went along to the bitter end with the attempts of dozens of originally Iberian families to prove their Aryan lineage.

Also, in the Netherlands, Mrs. Petra van den Boomgaard, a lawyer, is rounding up her exhaustive archival research into the dossiers of Calmeyer petitioners for her doctoral dissertation. She wants to probe the challenging question of what combination of circumstances led Jewish individuals and families to avail themselves of the opportunity to petition Calmeyer's office for a reassessment of their designation as Jews. It will be interesting to see whether she can establish a pattern. Meanwhile, she critically read through the manuscript for this book and suggested some helpful factual corrections.

Primarily thanks to Peter Niebaum's initiative and perseverance, the story of Hans Calmeyer is at long last becoming more widely known. By chance, this German lawyer found himself highly placed in the occupation government of the Netherlands, which enabled him to sabotage Hitler's Final Solution and save thousands of Jews living in that country, including my own family. Using his legal acumen to serve his standards of human decency, he created and maintained his own rescue operation, never slipping from his pose as a loyal German civil servant. So skillfully did he play this role in the very heart of the occupation government that some Holocaust interpreters later doubted the integrity of his motives.

Hans Calmeyer was a rare and genuine person: a German who, during Hitler's rule, clung to the ideals of human rights, justice, and tolerance. He despised Nazi doctrine and was, indeed, a righteous man among the nations, who deserves to be remembered and honored—not only by me and the families whose survival he made possible, but by everyone.

Dr. Martin Luther King, a strong opponent of the Vietnam War, said in his critical Riverside Church Address of April 4, 1967: "Even when pressed by demands of inner truth, men do not easily assume the task of opposing their government's policy, especially in time of war."

These words closely parallel Hans Calmeyer's declaration in Dutch internment quoted in chapter fifteen: "that a German, although he stands in the strongest opposition to the regime of his country, will not easily decide to sabotage his government's measures during a time of war. It requires a moral law much more compelling than solidarity with his country to turn his criticism into actual sabotage."

Yet, Calmeyer had bravely managed to chisel away at his government's murderous measures and in doing so had saved thousands of lives. Sadly, in post–World War II Germany, his enlightened ideas were up against the entrenched powerful forces that Dr. King warned against further along in his Riverside Church Address: "When machines and computers, profit motives and property rights are considered more important than people, the giant triplets of racism, extreme materialism, and militarism are incapable of being conquered."

We are now living in an epoch in which the nefarious triplets clearly have the upper hand. After all the decades of struggling for a better world, it is hard not to slip into despondency. Hans Calmeyer's low-key sabotage offers a model of resistance for people who will not surrender their integrity. For that I am grateful to him too!

Sources

❖ ❖ ❖

Cohen, Jaap. *De onontkoombare afkomst van Eli d'Oliveira. Een Portugees-Joodse familiegeschiedenis* (The inescapable ancestry of Eli d'Oliveira. A Portuguese-Jewish family history). Amsterdam: Querido, 2015.

De Jong, Louis. *De Bezetting* (The occupation). Amsterdam: Querido, 1985.

———. *Het Koninkrijk der Nederlanden in de Tweede Wereldoorlog* (The Kingdom of the Netherlands during World War II), 14 vols.; vol. 6, July 1942–May 1943, Gravenhage: Martinus Nijhoff, 1975.

Frank, Anne. *The Diary of Anne Frank: The Revised Critical Edition.* Prepared by the Netherlands' Institute for War Documentation. Edited by David Barnouw and Gerrold van der Stroom. Translated by Arnold J. Pomerans, B. M. Mooyaart, and Susan Massotty. New York: Doubleday, 2003.

Kempner, Robert M. W. *SS im Kreuzverhör* (SS under cross-examination), augmented 2nd ed. Nördlingen: GRENO, 1987.

Levy, Alan. *Nazi Hunter: The Wiesenthal File,* 2nd rev. ed. London: Constable and Robinson, 2006. First published in 1993.

Middelberg, Mathias. *Judenrecht, Judenpolitik und der Jurist Hans Calmeyer in den besetzten Niederlanden, 1940–1945* (Laws and policies against the Jews and the jurist Hans Calmeyer in the occupied Netherlands, 1940–1945). Göttingen: V & R unipress, 2005.

———. *Wer bin ich, dass ich über Leben und Tod entscheide? Hans Calmeyer, Rassenreferent in den Niederlanden 1941–1945* (Who am I that I should decide about life and death? Hans Calmeyer, in charge of race-related decisions in the Netherlands, 1941–1945). Göttingen: Wallstein, 2015.

Niebaum, Peter. *Ein Gerechter unter den Völkern. Hans Calmeyer in seiner Zeit (1903–1972)* (A righteous man among the nations. Hans Calmeyer in his time [1903–1972]). Osnabrück, Germany: Rasch, 2001.

———. *Hans Calmeyer—"ein anderer Deutscher" im 20. Jahrhundert* (Hans Calmeyer—a different kind of German in the twentieth century). Berlin: Frank & Timme, 2011.

Presser, Jacob. *Ashes in the Wind: The Destruction of Dutch Jewry,* translated by Arnold Pomerans. London: Souvenir Press, 1968. First published in the Netherlands in 1965 under the title *Ondergang* (Destruction).

Stenzel, Elke, editor. *Den Nazis eine schallende Ohrfeige versetzen* (Giving the Nazis a resounding slap in the face). Berlin: Frank & Timme, 2009.

Van den Boomgaard, Petra. "Legale ontduiking van de deportaties" ("Legal evasion of the deportations"). *Nederlands Juristenblad* (Dutch lawyers' journal), 44/45, December 18, 2015.

Van Galen-Herrmann, Ruth. *Calmeyer, dader of mensenredder? Visies op Calmeyers rol in de jodenvervolging* (Calmeyer, perpetrator or rescuer? Views of Calmeyer's role in the persecution of the Jews). Soesterberg, the Netherlands: Aspekt, 2009.

Von Frijtag Drabbe-Künzel, Geraldien. *Het geval Calmeyer* (The Calmeyer Case). Amsterdam: Mets & Schilt, 2008.

Warmbrunn, Werner. *The Dutch under German Occupation, 1940–1945.* Stanford, CA: Stanford University Press, 1963.

Weil, Grete. *Generationen* (Generations). Frankfurt, Main: Fischer, 1985.

Notes

✢ ✢ ✢

Chapter One: Early Childhood in Frankfurt

1. Stenzel, 226.

2. Minna Braun, "Die Prinzessin mit der Nas'," in *Jüdisches Jugendbuch 5,* eds. Emil B. Cohn and Ilse Rabin. Berlin: Jüdischer Verlag, 1935, 19–35.

Chapter Two: Hans Calmeyer

1. Niebaum, Ein anderer Deutscher, 69ff.

2. Ibid., 73ff.

3. Ibid., 79.

4. Niebaum, Ein Gerechter, 101.

5. Niebaum, Ein anderer Deutscher, 82.

6. Ibid., 87.

7. Ibid., 93.

8. Ibid., 94.

9. Ibid., 99–100.

10. Ibid., 100–101.

Chapter Three: Settling in the Netherlands
1. Van Galen-Herrmann, 20.
2. Niebaum, Ein anderer Deutscher, 12.

Chapter Four: The First Years of German Occupation
1. Presser, 11.
2. Ibid., 27–28.
3. Ibid., 49.
4. Shortly before and after the infamous 1938 *Anschluss*, Austria's union with Germany, Seyss-Inquart had served briefly as chancellor of Austria.
5. Niebaum, Ein Gerechter, 164.

Chapter Five: An Official at the Reich Commissariat
1. Niebaum, Ein anderer Deutscher, 12.
2. Presser, 34.
3. Niebaum, Ein anderer Deutscher, 18ff.
4. Van Galen-Herrmann, 58.
5. Middelberg, Wer bin ich, 65.
6. Van Galen-Herrmann, 59.
7. Middelberg, Wer bin ich, 79.
8. Ibid., 93ff.

Chapter Six: Wearing the Star of David
1. Stenzel, 242.
2. See URL at www.jewishvirtuallibrary.org/adolf-eichmann-letter-on-the-beginning-of-deportations-from-western-europe-June-1942.

Chapter Seven: Different Destinies
1. Middelberg, Judenrecht, Judenpolitik und der Jurist Hans Calmeyer, 2005.

Chapter Eight: Roundups
1. Niebaum, Ein anderer Deutscher, 30–31, derived from Warmbrunn, 172f.
2. Ibid., 21ff.
3. Ibid., 24ff.
4. Ibid., 26.
5. Niebaum, Ein Gerechter, 380.
6. Ibid., 177.
7. Niebaum, Ein anderer Deutscher, 40.
8. Middelberg, Wer bin ich, 123.
9. Niebaum, Ein anderer Deutscher, 32.

Chapter Nine: Sabotaging Hitler's Final Solution
1. Niebaum, Ein anderer Deutscher, 40.
2. Niebaum, Ein Gerechter, 179.
3. Niebaum, Ein anderer Deutscher, 46.
4. Ibid., 46–47.
5. Middelberg, Wer bin ich, 119.
6. Frank, 371.
7. Presser, 212–213, 383.
8. Niebaum, Ein anderer Deutscher, 28; Middelberg, Wer bin ich, 133–140.

Chapter Ten: The Tide Is Turning
1. De Jong, Het Koninkrijk, 700ff.
2. Niebaum, Ein anderer Deutscher, 34.
3. Von Frijtag Drabbe-Künzel, 215–217.
4. Niebaum, Ein anderer Deutscher, 40.
5. Middelberg, Wer bin ich, 102.
6. Van Galen-Herrmann, 61–62.
7. Niebaum, Ein anderer Deutscher, 48.
8. Middelberg, Wer bin ich, 79.

Chapter Eleven: Bolting Out of Reach
1. Stenzel, 263–264.

Chapter Twelve: Barograph
1. Middelberg, Wer bin ich, 125.
2. Niebaum, Ein anderer Deutscher, 52–53.

Chapter Thirteen: Hunger Winter
1. Niebaum, Ein anderer Deutscher, 53.
2. Stenzel, 283–286.
3. De Jong, De Bezetting, 772.

Chapter Fourteen: Liberation
1. Stenzel, 288–289.

Chapter Fifteen: In Detention
1. Middelberg, Wer bin ich, 177.
2. Niebaum, Ein anderer Deutscher, 51–52.
3. De Jong, Het Koninkrijk, 6, 309.
4. Niebaum, Ein anderer Deutscher, 57.
5. Ibid., 56.
6. Ibid.
7. Middelberg, Wer bin ich, 180–181.
8. Niebaum, Ein anderer Deutscher, 57.
9. Van Galen-Herrmann, 127–133.
10. Niebaum, Ein anderer Deutscher, 59–60.
11. Ibid., 57.
12. Ibid., 60.
13. Ibid., 55–56.

Chapter Sixteen: New Beginning
1. Niebaum, Ein anderer Deutscher, 189–191.

2. Ibid., 111.
3. Ibid., 112.
4. Ibid., 105.
5. Ibid., 106.
6. Ibid.

Chapter Seventeen: Denazification
1. Niebaum, Ein anderer Deutscher, 117–119.
2. Ibid., 120.
3. Niebaum, Ein Gerechter, 286.
4. Niebaum, Ein anderer Deutscher, 123.
5. Ibid., 121ff.
6. Ibid.
7. Niebaum, Ein Gerechter, 272.
8. Niebaum, Ein anderer Deutscher, 110.
9. Ibid.
10. Niebaum, Ein Gerechter, 284–285.

Chapter Eighteen: Where to Fit In?
1. Niebaum, Ein Gerechter, 302f.
2. Ibid., 308–310.
3. Niebaum, Ein anderer Deutscher, 112.
4. Ibid., 81.
5. Niebaum, Ein Gerechter, 305–306.
6. Ibid., 308–310.
7. Ibid., 311.
8. Niebaum, Ein anderer Deutscher, 116.
9. Ibid., 139.
10. Ibid., 136.
11. Ibid., 139.
12. Ibid., 116.

Chapter Twenty: Restoration
1. Niebaum, Ein anderer Deutscher, 122.
2. Ibid.
3. Ibid., 124.
4. Ibid., 127, Niebaum, Ein Gerechter, 328f.
5. Niebaum, Ein anderer Deutscher, 140.
6. Ibid., 128f.
7. Ibid., 131.
8. Ibid., 130.
9. Ibid., 132.

Chapter Twenty-three: Slightly Eccentric
1. In the early 1990s, after both his parents had died, Peter Calmeyer went through the family archive. In the process, he eliminated elements he considered "too compromising," largely excising Michael from the family record. As a result, available information about Hans Calmeyer's later life has large gaps where his second son was concerned. In March 2015, the author wrote to Michael, who lives in the U.S. and goes by the name Michael Calmeyer Hentschel, posing questions that only he could answer. Michael replied promptly and generously. In the later chapters of this book, all quotations from Michael Calmeyer Hentschel are drawn from this series of personal communications via email between March and August 2015. Michael and his three children are the only living descendants of Hans Calmeyer.
2. Niebaum, Ein anderer Deutscher, 132.
3. Ibid.
4. Quoted by Michael Calmeyer Hentschel on his website at www.hanscalmeyer.com.
5. Niebaum, Ein anderer Deutscher, 132.
6. Ibid., 130.
7. Ibid., 137.

8. Ibid., 140.

9. Ibid., 137.

10. Ibid.

11. Ibid., 137–138.

12. Ibid., 139.

13. Niebaum, Ein Gerechter, 366.

14. Niebaum, Ein anderer Deutscher, 138–140.

15. Levy, 157–158.

16. Niebaum, Ein anderer Deutscher, 141–142.

17. Niebaum, Ein Gerechter, 32–36.

18. Niebaum, Ein anderer Deutscher, 142.

Chapter Twenty-four: Too Little, Too Little!

1. Niebaum, Ein anderer Deutscher, 90.

2. Ibid., 145–148.

3. Ibid., 154.

4. Ibid., 150–152.

5. Ibid., 154.

6. Ibid.

Chapter Twenty-five: Academc and Real Life

1. Laureen Nussbaum, ed., *George Hermann. Unvorhanden und stumm, doch zu Menschen noch reden. Briefe aus dem Exil 1933–1941 an seine Tochter Hilde. Weltabschied, ein Essay* (Georg Hermann, "Not present and silent, yet still talking to people." Letters from exile to his daughter Hilde. "Farewell to the World," an essay), Mannheim, Germany: Persona, 1991.

2. Weil, 7.

3. Stenzel, 296–297.

4. See *Society and Natural Resources*, 17: "Community-Based Participatory Health Survey of Hanford, WA Downwinders: A Model for Citizen Empowerment," Rudi H. Nussbaum et al., 547–559, 2004.

5. Stenzel, 298.
6. Written by Downwinder Sara T. George, Vancouver, Washington, July 17, 1991.

Chapter Twenty-six: Wrestling the Past

1. Niebaum, Ein anderer Deutscher, 142ff.
2. Ibid., 146.
3. Ibid., 155–156.
4. Niebaum, Ein Gerechter, 48ff.
5. Ibid., 58.
6. Kempner, 197ff.
7. Niebaum, Ein anderer Deutscher, 160.
8. Ibid., 130f.
9. Ibid., 163.

Chapter Twenty-seven: Preparing for Death

1. Niebaum, Ein anderer Deutscher, 168f.
2. Ibid., 165.
3. Ibid., 169–171.
4. Email communications from Claus Cronemeyer to the author of October 5 and November 11, 2015, and telephone conversation of October 27, 2015.

Chapter Twenty-eight: A Circle Closes

1. Middelberg, Wer bin ich, 199.
2. Von Frijtag Drabbe-Künzel, 262–270.

Chapter Twenty-nine: A Devastating Loss

1. Nussbaum family memorabilia.
2. Van Galen-Herrmann, 23ff.
3. Ibid., 26.
4. Ibid., 169f.

Chapter Thirty: Fulfilling My Promise
1. Middelberg, Wer bin ich, 214–218.
2. Niebaum, Ein Gerechter, 340.

Acknowledgments
1. Anne Frank, *Liebe Kitty: Ihr Romanentwurf in Briefen* [Anne Frank, Dear Kitty: Her draft for an epistolary novel, with an afterword by Laureen Nussbaum], Berlin, Germany: Secession, May 2019.

Acknowledgments

✤ ✤ ✤

It was Peter Niebaum, a scholarly high school teacher in the Northern German city of Osnabrück who around 1990 first studied the amazing rescue action undertaken 50 years earlier by his fellow Osnabrücker, the lawyer Hans Calmeyer. Niebaum did the basic research and, in 2001, published an extensive biography, *Ein Gerechter unter den Völkern: Hans Calmeyer in seiner Zeit (1903–1972)*, followed by a shorter version in 2011, *Hans Calmeyer ein "anderer Deutscher" im 20. Jahrhundert*. Everything subsequently written about Hans Calmeyer both in German and in Dutch has been either a critical analysis or an elaboration of Niebaum's basic work. The present book is the first English text about Hans Calmeyer.

I owe warm thanks to the following Osnabrückers: to Peter Niebaum's widow Ursel and their children, Henrike and Rasmus, as well as to Ralf Steiner of the "Calmeyer Initiative" and to the historian Dr. Joachim Castan, custodian of the Calmeyer Archive. Their unstinting support has been essential. Dr. Mathias Middelberg, yet another Osnabrücker and member of the German parliament, wrote his doctoral dissertation in jurisprudence on Calmeyer's work in the occupied Netherlands. It was followed in 2015 by his very readable book for the general public *"Wer bin ich, dass ich über Leben und Tod entscheide?" Hans Calmeyer 'Rassen-referent' in den Niederlanden 1941–1945.* Dr. Middelberg most helpfully shared primary sources with me, including some pertaining to my own family's survival story. My most sincere appreciation for his generous cooperation.

The link up with all of these Osnabrückers is due to our dear friends, Klaus Muck, pediatrician, and his ever so hospitable wife, Eva, who over the last 30 years created a home-away-from-home for my husband and me in the outskirts of Osnabrück. I cannot even begin to thank them! They connected us to Peter Niebaum in the 1990s and more recently introduced me to Claus Cronemeyer, MD, the Osnabrück physician who cared for Hans Calmeyer's widow, Ruth, until her death in 1988. Over the years, Ruth Calmeyer had told her good doctor about her husband's secret rescue operation in the occupied Netherlands, and Doctor Cronemeyer had been the one who first called Peter Niebaum's attention to Hans Calmeyer's remarkable story. I owe Doctor Cronemeyer many thanks for the fine interview we had in 2013 and for his generous written information.

I am also very grateful to the archaeologist Dr. Ursula Seidl-Calmeyer, widow of Hans and Ruth Calmeyer's son Peter. She is not from Osnabrück yet belongs indirectly to her husband's hometown. Dr. Seidl-Calmeyer helpfully called my attention to a new book about the fate of the "Portuguese Jews" of the Netherlands during the German occupation: Jaap Cohen, *De onontkoombare afkomst van Eli d'Oliveira, een Portugees-Joodse familie-geschiedenis.* In Cohen's study, Hans Calmeyer's sustained efforts to save the lives of this very special segment of the Dutch population figures prominently. I might have missed it without Dr. Seidl-Calmeyer's hint!

The Osnabrück Calmeyer people brought me in touch with the Dutch lawyer-historian Petra van den Boomgaard with whom I linked up in 2017. In April 2019 Petra defended her doctoral dissertation about Hans Calmeyer's rescue work in the Netherlands, based on extensive research in the Dutch archives. She gave my manuscript a critical reading, and I am very grateful for her helpful remarks and suggestions. Her dissertation will be published later this year by Verbum in Hilversum, the Netherlands under the title, *Voor de nazis geen Jood* [Not a Jew for the Nazis].

Another important person I got in contact with via the Osnabrückers is Michael Calmeyer Hentschel, Hans Calmeyer's second son, who has lived in the United States since 1963. Born out of wedlock in the city of Goslar, he has been shunted aside by the respectable Osnabrück family. Yet, Michael happened to be the last person Hans Calmeyer spoke to before his untimely death in 1972. Michael was extraordinarily generous with his time, answering my many questions with pages full of helpful details for which I cannot thank him enough.

The recent flurry of publicity surrounding my participation in the launch of Anne Frank's epistolary novel[1] brought me a surprise email. Christian Wurl, who identified himself as a nephew of Ruth Labusch Calmeyer, sent me precious memories of Hans and Ruth Calmeyer spanning over thirty years. Alas, they came too late for this book, yet, Mr. Wurl deserves my gratitude for sharing his reminiscences.

Since I wanted to introduce Calmeyer's story to readers of English, I originally set out to translate Peter Niebaum's shorter Calmeyer biography from German. In the process it became more and more obvious, that Niebaum's text was not geared to the American public. I asked my good friend Ursula LeGuin for advice. She referred me to a former colleague, Dr. Tony Wolk, professor of English at Portland State University, where I taught German language and literature for many years.

Since I was daunted by the prospect of adapting Niebaum's text to American and worldwide anglophones, he suggested that I consult Karen Kirtley, an experienced editor.

Karen was very willing to work with me, but she insisted that I interweave my own tale of survival and that of my family with Calmeyer's story. Both Ursula LeGuin and Tony Wolk heartily supported that idea, so Karen and I set to work with ever so many attachments containing sections or whole chapters flying back and forth between Karen's home in Portland and mine in Seattle. Karen's contributions to this book are invaluable both in the text itself and with regard to the nitty-gritty of preparing a clean-looking manuscript, including the tedious end notes. I cannot thank you enough, Karen, even though the present hybrid biography/memoir landed our book in an uneasy spot between two categories!

Academic presses turned down our manuscript because the free-floating memoir sections did not fit their agenda, and for other publishers our text with its many end notes was "too academic." Luckily my friend Mary Fillmore, who had just published her fascinating World War II novel *An Address in Amsterdam* with She Writes, urged us to submit our manuscript to that press, because of the good experiences she'd had with them. I followed her advice and was referred to Bridget Boland of *New Muse* for developmental editing. Bridget was good to work with, and I'm grateful for her streamlining our text by fusing its two main strands more tightly together. Several beta readers: Mary Fillmore, Jim Boland, Karen Kirtley, our son Fred and his wife, Nan, gave the manuscript a much-appreciated final critical reading, and once their suggestions were incorporated, off it went, to be published by She Writes Press. Both Fred and Nan had recommended that I bring the final chapter up to date regarding the startling parallels between the political and social situation in the present-day US and that of Germany at the end of the Weimar Republic. I gratefully followed their advice. Thanks to Fred I was able to insert the pictures into the text, which I could not do by myself.

Fred and Nan have not been the only family members drawn into my "Calmeyer project." Son Ralph has consistently been on emergency stand-by whenever my limited computer skills woefully failed me, which happened only too often. His son-in-law, Jesse Willard, helped me with fulfilling the publicity demands by updating the entry Wikipedia had under my name. Heartfelt thanks to the two of them. The rest of the family and my many friends close by and far away, as well as my co-residents here in Seattle at University House shall be relieved when I will no longer be preoccupied with "the book." I'm grateful for their faith in me as well as for their abiding encouragement.

My friends Ronald Leopold and Menno Metselaar of the Anne Frank House in Amsterdam have been most supportive over the years. They found me the cover picture for the book and nego-tiated its use with the Dutch Institute for War Documentation.

The help of the head librarian of the Wallingford branch of the superb Seattle Public Library System, Dawn Rutherford, was much appreciated. She was very efficient in providing me with a list of books I could use as comparative texts for pub-licity purposes. Thanks also to author Donna Cameron, who just published *A Year of Living Kindly* with She Writes Press. She recommended the publicity firm *JKS* to me. I am looking forward to working with them in the coming months.

Last but not least, my profound gratitude to Ted Koppel for his fine personal introduction to *Shedding Our Stars* based on a friendship that goes back 70 years. To Dr. Jack Boas, Dr. Gayle Greene, Dr. Penny Milbouer, Dr. Tony Wolk, Mary Fill-more, Ronald Leopold, and Dr. Elizabeth Minnich, my deep appreciation for their supportive blurbs. Most of them read previous versions of the manuscript and made valuable suggestions. Each of their statements comes from a different perspective, which makes me anticipate that the book may be relevant to a great variety of readers. What more can I hope for?

My life's partner, Rudi, was no longer alive when I worked on the book, but I often invoked his helpful, steadying presence from the far beyond.

About the Authors

Author photo © Klaus Muck

Born in 1927 in Frankfurt, **Laureen Nussbaum** was the middle daughter of the Klein family. When she was eight, the Kleins left Hitler's Germany and settled in Amsterdam, close to Anne Frank and her family, old friends from Frankfurt. After Hans Calmeyer, the German official in charge of "dubious cases," decided in favor of their petition to be considered non-Jews, and Nussbaum, her mother and sisters were allowed to shed their yellow stars, her father, living in a "privileged mixed marriage," was not deported. In 1957, Nussbaum and her husband, Rudi, moved to the United States and eventually, raised their family

in Portland, OR, where Rudi joined the physics department of
Portland State University. There, Nussbaum went back to school
and subsequently got her PhD in German Language and Literature at the University of Washington. She joined the faculty
of PSU, published dozens of academic papers, and eventually,
retired as a full professor. In 2012, after her husband's death,
she moved to Seattle.

KAREN KIRTLEY is a freelance editor and writer and avid music
lover. She served as editorial director of Amadeus Press for several
years, where she helped journalist Richard Newman put together
the breathtaking biography, *Alma Rosé: Vienna to Auschwitz*,
(Amadeus Press, 2000). Kirtley lives in Portland, OR.

PHOTO CREDITS

✤ ✤ ✤

Front cover: Amsterdam, June 20, 1943. Photo by Herman Heukels, photographer for the Nazi weekly *Storm SS*. Source and permission: *Beeldbank WO 2,* Dutch Institute for War Documentation.

Pages 27, 30, 32, 42, 128, 178, 185, 209: Hans Calmeyer photos supplied by *Filmkontor Dr. Joachim Castan,* Osnabrück and reprinted with their permission.

Pages 39 and 40: photos of Margot Frank and Anne Frank supplied by the Anne Frank House in Amsterdam and reprinted with their permission.

Page 220: photo by Peter Schütte, freelance photographer in Portland, OR, reprinted with his permission.

Page 226: Middelberg book cover reprinted with the permission of Wallstein publishers, Göttingen, Germany.

Author headshot and all other photos in the book are part of the author's private family collection.

Selected Titles from She Writes Press

She Writes Press is an independent publishing company founded to serve women writers everywhere. Visit us at www.shewritespress.com.

When a Toy Dog Became a Wolf and the Moon Broke Curfew: A Memoir by Hendrika de Vries. $16.95, 978-1631526589. Hendrika is "Daddy's little girl," but when Nazis occupy Amsterdam and her father is deported to a POW labor camp, she must bond with her mother—who joins the Resistance after her husband's deportation—and learn about female strength in order to discover the strong woman she can become.

At the Narrow Waist of the World: A Memoir by Marlena Maduro Baraf. $16.95, 978-1631525889. In this lush and vivid coming-of-age memoir about a mother's mental illness and the healing power of a loving Jewish and Hispanic extended family, young Marlena must pull away from her mother, leave her Panama home, and navigate the transition to an American world.

Surviving the Survivors: A Memoir by Ruth Klein. $16.95, 978-1-63152-471-4. With both humor and deep feeling, Klein shares the story of her parents—who survived the Holocaust but could not overcome the tragedy they had experienced—and their children, who became indirect victims of the atrocities endured by the generation before them.

Jumping Over Shadows: A Memoir by Annette Gendler. $16.95, 978-1-63152-170-6. Like her great-aunt Resi, Annette Gendler, a German, fell in love with a Jewish man—but unlike her aunt, whose marriage was destroyed by "the Nazi times," Gendler found a way to make her impossible love survive.

Rethinking Possible: A Memoir of Resilience by Rebecca Faye Smith Galli. $16.95, 978-1-63152-220-8. After her brother's devastatingly young death tears her world apart, Becky Galli embarks upon a quest to recreate the sense of family she's lost—and learns about healing and the transformational power of love over loss along the way.

The Beauty of What Remains: Family Lost, Family Found by Susan Johnson Hadler. $16.95, 978-1-63152-007-5. Susan Johnson Hadler goes on a quest to find out who the missing people in her family were—and what happened to them—and succeeds in reuniting a family shattered for four generations.